THE STREETS WERE PAVED WITH GOLD

A PICTORIAL HISTORY OF THE KLONDIKE GOLD RUSH, 1896-1899

THE STREETS WERE PAVED WITH GOLD

a pictorial history of the klondike gold rush 1896-1899

by stan cohen

THE PROSPECTOR

LIBRARY OF CONGRESS
CATALOG CARD NO. 77-80011

ISBN 978-0-933126-03-9

First Printing: July 1977

Revised Edition:
First Printing: April 1987
Thirteenth Printing: April 2005
Fourteenth Printing: March 2007
Fifteenth Printing: March 2009

Printed in Canada
by Friesens Corporation, Altona, Manitoba

ABOUT THE AUTHOR

STAN COHEN, a native of West Virginia, is a graduate geologist and spent two summers working in Alaska as a geologist for the U.S. Forest Service. Since 1976 he has spent part of every summer in Alaska and the Yukon researching and writing about the North Country. He established Pictorial Histories Publishing Company in 1976 and has since written 79 history books and published over 300. His North Country titles include: *Gold Rush Gateway: Skagway and Dyea, Alaska; The Forgotten War; The Trail of '42; The White Pass and Yukon Route; Yukon River Steamboats; Rails Across the Tundra; Klondike Centennial Scrapbook; The Alaska Flying Expedition* and *Queen City of the North.* He and his wife, Anne, live in Missoula, Montana.

PICTORIAL HISTORIES PUBLISHING COMPANY, INC.
713 South Third Street West, Missoula, Montana 59801
PHONE (406) 549-8488   FAX (406) 728-9280
EMAIL phpc@montana.com
www.pictorialhistoriespublishing.com

INTRODUCTION

One of the most exciting chapters in the history of North America was written more than 2,000 miles from civilization. The time was the late 1890s and the event was the Klondike Gold Rush in the Yukon Territory of Canada.

The Western Hemisphere experienced gold rushes from the time of the 16th Century Spanish adventures in Latin America to the last rush in Alaska in the early 1900s. The history of the western United States and Canada was greatly influenced by the search for gold. No one can say how long it might have taken to settle these lands if prospectors had not led the way.

No gold rush in history could match the Klondike Rush of 1896-99 in the almost insane drive of people to conquer distance and weather conditions to reach the rich deposits of placer gold in the frozen, barren area of the Klondike River.

By the 1890s news could be flashed around the world rapidly, and the mass exodus to the Klondike gold fields was completed in just one year.

Human nature has really not changed much through the years. The uranium rush to the American West in the 1950s was the same sort of instant madness that characterized the Klondike. The next great precious metal strike might occur in the jungles of Africa, Brazil or New Guinea, and people would probably act in much the same way—assuming that government controls and world politics did not restrain them.

This book compares scenes of the gold rush period with the same scenes today. I have included many early pictures to tell the story as completely as possible. Time and mankind have not been kind to the sites and artifacts of the period, but it is surprising how much remains. Government agencies in the United States and Canada have preserved some of the history of the period.

Many good books have been written about this period and I urge the reader to search them out. It was a fascinating time. It should not be forgotten.

STAN COHEN

Dedicated to
all the men and women who
went looking for their "Eldorado."

ACKNOWLEDGMENTS & PHOTO IDENTIFICATION

I wish to thank the personnel at the Yukon Archives in Whitehorse, the Alaska Historical Library at Juneau, the University of Alaska Archives, the University of Washington Library, Special Collections in Seattle, the Anchorage Museum of History and Art, and Dedman's Photo Shop in Skagway, Alaska, for help in obtaining the original photos. The tourist bureaus in Whitehorse and Juneau and the White Pass and Yukon Railway helped with some of the new pictures. Many people, especially my wife, Anne, helped during the trip to the Yukon and Alaska during the summer of 1976. A special thanks to Bob McGiffert, who edited my manuscript; Gordon Lemon, Al Dekmar and Sherry Lierman, who printed the new photos and Joe Boddy, who did the art work.

The early photos in this book were gathered from various sources in the United States and Canada and are identified by the source, the photographer's last name when known and the year taken when known. Most of the modern pictures were taken by the author and his wife on their many trips north since 1976. Sources of other pictures are acknowledged in captions.

These abbreviations are used:
PABC—Provincial Archives of British Columbia
UAA—University of Alaska Archives, Fairbanks
AHL—Alaska Historical Library, Juneau
YA—Yukon Archives, Whitehorse
UW—University of Washington Special
    Collections, Seattle
D—Dedman's Photo Shop, Skagway
AMHA—Anchorage Museum of History and Art
NPS—National Park Service
The following photographers' works were used in this book:
Adams and Larkin
Banks, H.D.
Cantwell, George G.
Case and Draper
Child, ——
Curtis, Asahel
Doody, J.
Ellingsen, E.O.
Gillis, A.J.
Goetzman, H.J.
Hegg, E.A.
Hester, Wilhem
Lane, T.R.
Larss and Duclos
LaRoche, Henry
Prather, ——
Sarvant, Henry
Vogee, Arthur

TABLE OF CONTENTS

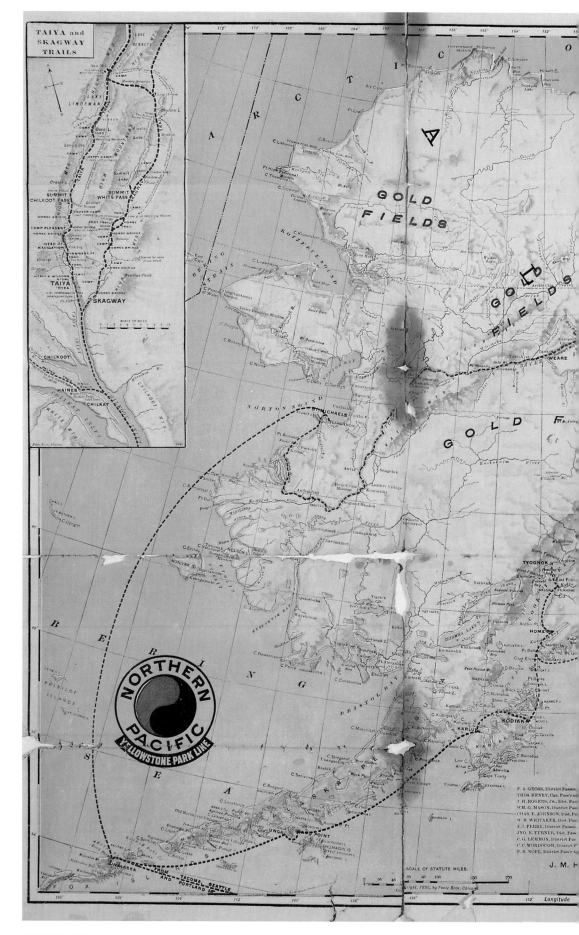

UNITED STATES PLACER MINING LAW.

[Prepared from the Revised Statutes of the United States.]

The term "placer claim," as defined by the supreme court of the United States, is: "Ground within defined boundaries which contains mineral in its earth, sand or gravel; ground that includes valuable deposits not in place, that is, not fixed in rock, but which are in a loose state, and may in most cases be collected by washing or amalgamation without milling."

The manner of locating placer mining claims differs from that of locating claims upon veins or lodes. In locating a vein or lode claim, the United States statutes provide that no claim shall extend more than 300 feet on each side of the middle of the vein at the surface, or 1,500 feet along the vein, and that no claim shall be limited by mining regulations to less than twenty-five feet on each side of the middle of the vein at the surface. In locating claims called "placer," however, the law provides that no location of such claim upon surveyed lands shall include more than twenty acres for each individual claimant. The supreme court, however, has held that one individual can hold as many locations as he can purchase and rely upon his possessory title; that a separate patent for each location is unnecessary.

Locators, however, have to show proof of citizenship or intention to become citizens. This may be done in the case of an individual by his own affidavit; in the case of an association incorporated by a number of individuals, by the affidavit of their authorized agent, made on his own knowledge or upon information and belief; and in the case of a company organized under the laws of any state or territory, by the filing of a certified copy of the charter or certificate of incorporation.

A patent for any land claimed and located may be obtained in the following manner: "Any person, association or corporation authorized to locate a claim, having claimed and located a piece of land, and who has or have

complied with the terms of the law, may file in the proper land office an application for a patent under oath, showing such compliance, together with a plat and field notes of the claim or claims in common made by or under the direction of the United States surveyor general, showing accurately the boundaries of the claim or claims, which shall be distinctly marked by monuments on the ground, and shall post a copy of such plat, together with a notice of such application for a patent, in a conspicuous place on the land embraced in such plat, previous to the application for a patent on such plat; and shall file an affidavit of at least two persons that such notice has been duly posted, and shall file a copy of the notice in such land office; and shall thereupon be entitled to a patent to the land in the manner following: The registrar of such land office, upon the filing of such application, plat, field notes, notices and affidavits, shall publish a notice that such application has been made, for a period of sixty days, in a newspaper to be by him designated, as published nearest to such claim; and he shall post such notice in his office for the same period. The claimant at the time of filing such application, or at any time thereafter, within sixty days of publication, shall file with the registrar a certificate of the United States surveyor general that $500 worth of labor has been expended or improvements made upon the claim by himself or grantors; that the plat is correct, with such further description by reference to natural objects or permanent monuments as shall identify the claim and furnish an accurate description to be incorporated in the patent. At the expiration of the sixty days of publication, the claimant shall file his affidavit showing that the plat and notice have been posted in a conspicuous place on the claim during such period of publication.

If no adverse claim shall have been filed with

the registrar of the land office at the expiration of said sixty days, the claimant is entitled to a patent upon the payment to the proper officer of $5 per acre in the case of a lode claim, and $2.50 per acre for a placer.

The location of a placer claim and keeping possession thereof until a patent shall be issued are subject to local laws and customs.

HOW TO MAKE AN ADVERSE CLAIM.

When an adverse claim is made during the sixty days period of publication, it must be under oath of the person or persons making the same, and shall show the nature, boundaries and extent of such adverse claim; and all proceedings, except publication of notice and filing affidavits thereof, are stayed until the controversy is settled by a court of competent jurisdiction or the adverse claim is waived. Within thirty days after filing adverse claim, contesting party shall begin proceedings to determine the question of right of possession, and shall prosecute the same with reasonable diligence to final judgment. Failure so to do operates as a waiver. After such judgment, the party entitled to possession may file with the registrar a certified copy of the judgment roll, together with a certificate from the surveyor general that the requisite amount of labor has been done on the claim and the description required in other cases, and shall pay to the registrar $5 per acre of such claim, whereupon the whole proceedings and judgment roll shall be certified by the registrar to the general land commissioner and the patent issues.

BEFORE WHOM OATHS MAY BE TAKEN.

All affidavits required under the mining laws of the United States may be made before any officer authorized to administer oaths within the land district where the claim may be situated, and all proofs may be taken before any such officer.

THE

NDIKE GOLD FIELDS
MAP OF
ALASKA

ENERAL AND DISTRICT PASSENGER AGENTS NORTHERN PACIFIC RAILWAY.

E.A. Hegg was the most prolific photographer of the gold rush. Originally from Bellingham, Washington, he headed north with the main wave of prospectors, crossed the Chilkoot Pass and floated down the Yukon to Dawson City. All the while he was hauling all his fragile photographic equipment. His studio in Skagway was located in the present Dedman's Photo Shop. Hegg documented every aspect of the Klondike rush from Seattle north and also participated in the Nome rush. After 20 years in the North, he returned to Bellingham. Years later, part of his remarkable collection was saved from destruction by Ethel Anderson Becker and preserved for future generations. YA

William Case and Horace Draper were early Alaska photographers who first set up their business in Skagway in a tent but later moved on to a more permanent location on Broadway.
YA MACBRIDE MUSEUM COLLECTION

H.C. Barley, originally from Denver, was hired by the new White Pass Co. in 1898 to document the company's railroad from Skagway, over the White Pass to Whitehorse. Barley stayed in Skagway for two years and left a remarkable record of the railroad and life during the gold rush. His first studio was on Fourth Avenue and in 1899 he moved onto Broadway next to The Pillbox Drug Co. YA BARLEY COLLECTION

Arthur Vogee's photo studio in Skagway.
YA VOGEE COLLECTION

The year 1896 began on a somber note. A depression in the United States had lingered since the silver panic of 1893. The West Coast was hit especially hard, with many layoffs in the timber industries. The frontier had been conquered and thousands of men were roaming the country looking for their own "El Dorado." Some found it.

Up in Alaska and the Yukon, a country as remote as the moon to most people, things were beginning to happen. Alaska was just beginning to show the promise of mineral wealth that was to justify "Seward's Folly" of 1867. Several major gold deposits had been found in the Juneau area and placer gold had been found in other places. Towns like Circle were commercial centers for the hundreds of miners working along the Yukon River. In Canada, placer gold had been found on Fortymile River in 1887, and the town that was built there became the major trading post in the Yukon. Hundreds of other miners were strung out along the streams that fed the Yukon River in the late 1880s and early 1890s. Gold had also been discovered earlier in the Cassier area of British Columbia and the entire North country was becoming important for mineral production.

One problem in the area was the dispute between the United States and Canada over location of the Alaska-Yukon boundary. The first attempt to establish a boundary occurred in 1869 when it was discovered that the old Hudson's Bay fort at Fort Yukon was actually in Alaska and not Canada. William Ogilvie of the Canadian government made surveys in the 1880s to try to establish a line and in 1896 both countries agreed on a line near the town of Fortymile. The line along the coast was not fixed until after the

William Ogilvie was the official surveyor for the Canadian government and surveyed the boundary between Alaska and the Yukon. He had the reputation of being the most honest man in the North, never wanting any personal gain for himself, and was named the Commissioner of the Yukon in 1898. UW

gold rush had begun. Canada wanted a tidewater port so people could reach the interior without going through American territory. The Canadian government thought it could extend its authority to Skagway and Dyea, but ended up agreeing to a border at the two mountain passes leading into the interior—White and Chilkoot. There it remains today, 15 miles from tidewater.

Three men instrumental in the early development of the North were Arthur Harper, Al Mayo and LeRoy Napoleon (Jack) McQuesten. They had formed a limited partnership with each

Circle City, Alaska, in the 1890s. This was an important mining and trading camp on the Yukon River before the gold rush, and was the starting point for many of the early claim stakers in the Klondike. It was built by Jack McQuesten, a leading trader in the Yukon area for many years. UW CURTIS

View of Fortymile in the 1890s. Situated at the confluence of the Fortymile and Yukon Rivers, it was the major town in the Yukon and the scene of the first major gold rush in the area in the 1880s. After the Klondike strike, the town and surrounding creeks were almost abandoned. AHL

The remains of Fortymile are now accessible by a four-mile walk from the road leading into the abandoned mining town of Clinton Creek 60 miles northwest of Dawson, or by riverboat.

other and the Alaska Commercial Company to trade in the area. For many years before the gold rush, they traveled the Yukon Valley and established trading posts which grew to great importance when the actual rush started.

For years people had thought that there was a great concentration of gold somewhere in the Yukon but it was a quirk of fate that led to discovery of the Klondike.

There are several versions of the story of the discovery of gold. One of the more believable is this:

Robert Henderson, a long-time prospector in the North, had found some color on Gold Bottom Creek near present day Bonanza Creek (Rabbit Creek). He met George Carmack, a white man who had married an Indian and adopted Indian ways, and two of his Indian relatives, Tagish Charley and Skookum Jim, at the mouth of the Klondike River. As was the custom of the prospectors in the area, Henderson told Carmack about his discovery and suggested that Carmack do some prospecting. Henderson had no love for Indians and suggested that Carmack stake a claim alone. This remark cost Henderson the wealth that had eluded him for years.

Carmack and the two Indians half-heartedly trudged up Rabbit Creek prospecting as they went. They found nothing until they made camp on the creek the night of August 16, 1896. When they panned at this campsite they found a quantity of gold. They were entitled to their vision of great wealth, for they had discovered one of the greatest concentrations of placer gold in the world.

The next day they staked their claims and started for Fortymile to record them. Either in their haste to get to Fortymile or because of Henderson's prejudice against Indians, the three did not stop to tell Henderson of their discovery. Henderson was to learn of it only after most of the creeks had been staked.

Carmack made it back to Fortymile, recorded his claim and spread the news of his discovery. At first no one believed him, but careful examination of the gold showed that it had not come from any known claim in the area, and the rush was on. In a matter of days the news spread up

THE MEN WHO STARTED IT ALL

Robert Henderson. UW

Skookum Jim. YA

George Carmack. UW

Tagish Charley. YA

George Carmack, Tagish Charley and Skookum Jim dance a jig with their pan after discovering gold on Rabbit Creek (now called Bonanza Creek) on August 17, 1896. It was the beginning of the greatest gold rush in history. BODDY

and down the creeks, and the towns along the Yukon River were deserted.

It was almost a year before word reached the outside world, and by that time most of the creeks in the Klondike had been staked by the prospectors on the scene.

The gold was found along the tributaries of the Klondike River which flowed westward, meeting the Yukon River at Dawson.

FORM A.

for Placer

APPLICATION AND AFFIDAVIT ~~OF DISCOVERER OF QUARTZ~~ MINE.

I, G. W. Carmack
of Forty Mile
hereby apply, under the Dominion Lands Mining Regulations, for a mining location in

a Creek known as Bonanza Creek flowing into Klondike River.

Discovery claim on Bonanza Creek.

for the purpose of mining for *Gold*
and I hereby solemnly swear :—

1. That I have discovered therein a deposit of *Gold*

2. That I am, to the best of my knowledge and belief the first discoverer of the said deposit.

3. That I am unaware that the land is other than vacant Dominion land. ✓

4. That I did, on the *17th* day of *August* 1896, mark out on the ground, in accordance in every particular with the provisions of ~~subsection (a) of section four of~~ the said Mining Regulations, the location for which I make this application; and that in so doing I did not encroach on any mining location previously laid out by any other person.

5. That the said mining location contains, as nearly as I could measure or estimate, an area of
acres, and that the description and (sketch, if any) of this date hereto attached, signed by , set forth in detail, to the best of knowledge and ability, its position, form and dimensions.

6. That I make this application in good faith to acquire the land for the sole purpose of mining to be prosecuted by myself or by myself and associates, or by my assigns.

Sworn before me at Ft. Constantine
this 24th day of September
1896 C. Constantine
a city [....]

G. W. Carmack

NOTE In case of abandoned ground it may be necessary to omit No. 2.

Form No. 109.

George Carmack's placer gold claim file for his discovery on Bonanza Creek (Rabbit Creek), August 17, 1896.

THE SEATTLE POST-INTELLIGENCER.

VOL. XXXII, NO. 62 — SEATTLE, WASHINGTON, SATURDAY, JULY 17, 1897. — EIGHT-PAGE EDITION.

LATEST NEWS FROM THE KLONDIKE.
9 O'CLOCK EDITION.

GOLD! GOLD! GOLD! GOLD!

Sixty-Eight Rich Men on the Steamer Portland.

STACKS OF YELLOW METAL!

Some Have $5,000, Many Have More, and a Few Bring Out $100,000 Each.

THE STEAMER CARRIES $700,000.

Special Tug Chartered by the Post-Intelligencer to Get the News.

The Latest Reports From the New Eldorado Arrive This Morning—Interviews With Those Who Have Come Down From the North With New-Found Fortunes—The Recent Strikes Seem to Be as Rich as Reported—There Is Plenty of Gold, But Only the Hardy and Provident Can Secure It—No Man Who Is Without a Suitable Outfit Should Attempt Fortune in That Remote Region—There Will No Doubt Be a Great Rush for the New Discoveries, and the Majority Will Outfit in and Leave From Seattle.

The Post-Intelligencer chartered a tug at Port Townsend last night to enable a staff correspondent to meet the incoming steamship Portland, from St. Michael, loaded with her treasure of $700,000 from the Klondike.

The steamship was boarded at 2 o'clock

steamed, so the tug was ordered sent to Seattle with the correspondent on board.

BRINGING BACK GOLD.

Sixty-eight Miners on the Portland Confirm the Fabulous Stories.

ON BOARD STEAMSHIP PORTLAND, 2 a. m.—At 2 o'clock this morning the steamship Portland, from St. Michael, for Seattle, passed up Sound with more than a ton of solid gold on board and 68 passengers.

THE LAND OF GOLD.

Map Showing the Yukon Country, With Klondike and Bonanza Creeks, Where the Recent Rich Discoveries Have Been Made. The Overland Route From Seattle, by Dyea, Chilkoot Pass, the Lakes and River, Is Shown, as Well as the Outside Route by the Way of Bering Sea. St. Michaels and the Yukon River. The Dotted Line Shows the International Boundary.

On July 16, 1897, the Alaska Commercial Company's ship *Excelsior* docked in San Francisco with the first news of the gold strike. The next day the North American Trading and Transportation Company's ship *Portland* docked at Seattle with 68 miners and gold reportedly worth more than $700,000. The gold strike was confirmed. It was said that the gold fields were rich beyond anyone's wildest dreams. As the news spread around the world, people quit their jobs, took their savings, left their families and headed for the "Promised Land."

Seattle, with a population of 67,000, was the largest city along the North Coast and was the natural jumping-off point for the stampeders. During the gold rush its population swelled many times, even though it lost 10,000 of its own citizens to the stampede.

The ship *Excelsior* docking at San Francisco on July 16, 1897. It brought the first news of the gold strike to the outside world and together with the docking of the *Portland* in Seattle started one of the greatest gold rushes in history.
UM CANTWELL, 1897, RICHARD MOLL, FREEPORT, ILLINOIS

Steamer *Portland* passing through the Gulf of Alaska on the way to Seattle with the news of the great gold discovery in the North. BETTMANN ARCHIVE/NEW YORK

The *Portland*, docked in Seattle on July 17, 1897, with gold reported to be worth $700,000 and prospectors who spread the news of the great "Eldorado" around the world.

In the summer of 1897, Seattle became the most important city on the West Coast for supplying the thousands of people heading for the Klondike. The streets were literally overflowing with goods waiting to be bought by the gold-crazed prospectors.

KLONDYKE Don't get excited and rush away only half prepared. You are going to a country where grub is more valuable than gold and frequently can't be bought for any price. We can fit you out quicker and better than any firm in town. We have had lots of experience, know how to pack and what to furnish.

COOPER & LEVY

NOS. 104 AND 106 FIRST AVENUE SOUTH.

Polk's City Directory for Seattle said this in 1898:

Since the last issue of this directory the commercial conditions of Seattle have undergone a radical change; an era of unexpected prosperity in a measure incident to the Klondike gold excitement has swept over the city. Just as the city was slowly recovering from the dull times due to the panic of 93-94 the news of the Alaska gold discoveries flashed throughout the world, and Seattle, being as geographically situated that she was immediately recognized as the gateway to the new Eldorado, at once became the scene of unexpected activity, and capital commenced to pour into the city from unexpected sources for investment.

Most people believed that the Klondike was in Alaska and many books and pamphlets during the period placed it there. It did not take people long to realize that they would have to cross into a foreign country to "strike it rich."

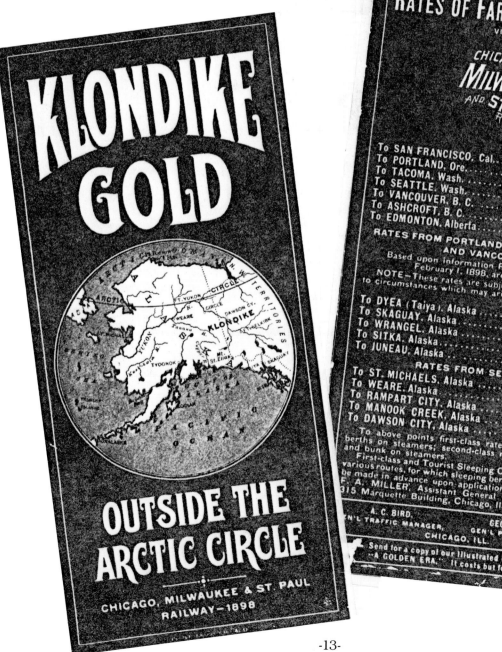

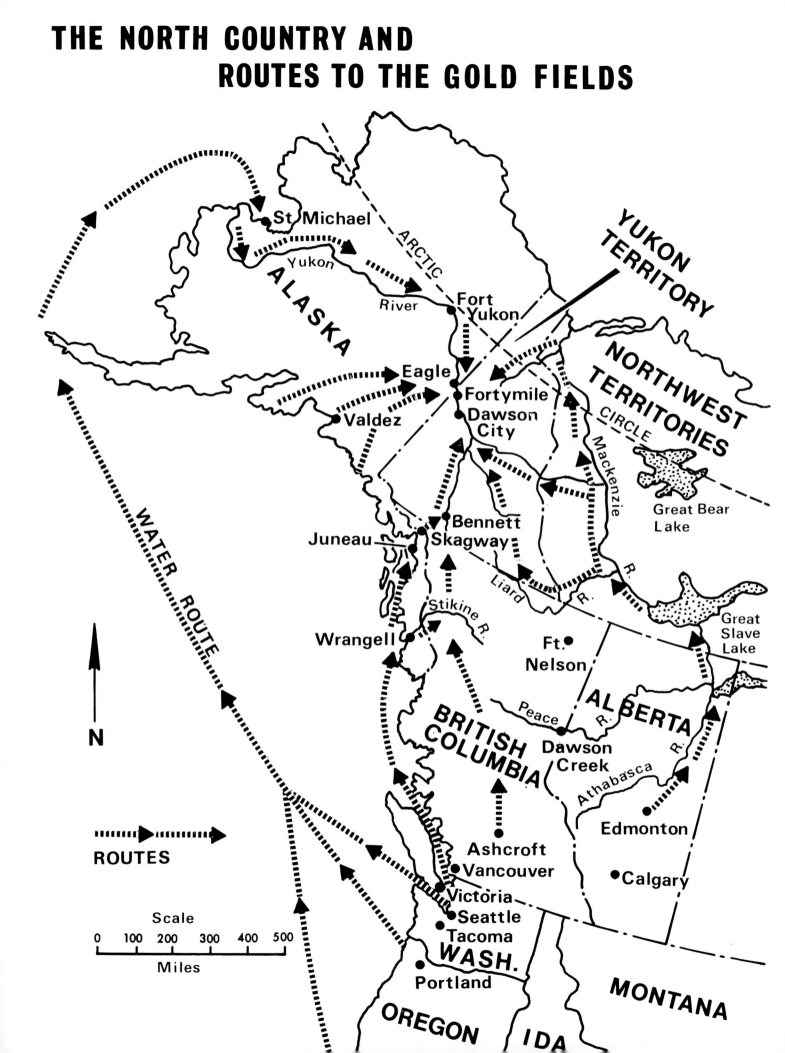

THE NORTH COUNTRY AND ROUTES TO THE GOLD FIELDS

YUKON TERRITORY

NORTHWEST TERRITORIES

St Michael

ALASKA

Yukon River

ARCTIC

Fort Yukon

CIRCLE

Mackenzie R.

Great Bear Lake

Eagle

Valdez

Fortymile

Dawson City

Bennett

Juneau

Skagway

Great Slave Lake

Liard R.

Stikine R.

Wrangell

Ft. Nelson

BRITISH COLUMBIA

ALBERTA

Peace R.

Dawson Creek

Athabasca R.

WATER ROUTE

N

Edmonton

Ashcroft

Vancouver

Victoria

Calgary

Seattle

Tacoma

WASH.

Portland

MONTANA

OREGON

IDA

- - ▶ - - ▶
ROUTES

Scale
0 100 200 300 400 500
Miles

Many guide books were published in 1897 and 1898 to capitalize on the thousands of stampeders heading for their "Eldorado."
AUTHOR'S COLLECTION

The main street of
Wrangell, Alaska, one of
the stopping points along
the Inside Passage Way
to Skagway and Dyea.
One of the routes to
Dawson, up the Stikine
River, started here.
FROM A STEREOSCOPE VIEW

Juneau, Alaska, was the
largest and most impor-
tant town on the Inside
Passage Way from the
West Coast to Skagway
and Dyea—the starting
points for the overland
trails to the Yukon River.
It was a bustling mining
town in its own right and
also an important outfit-
ting point. AHL 1897

Juneau is the capital of
Alaska and an important
government and trade
center for Southeast
Alaska, with a population
of more than 15,000.

Other cities up and down the coast—San Francisco, Portland, Tacoma, and Vancouver and Victoria, British Columbia—were also trying to cash in on the great excitement. In the spring of 1898, 112 ships were being built to meet the demand for passage north. Every available boat, steamer and barge on the West Coast was pressed into service. Some of these were derelicts that had a hard time staying afloat, but no one cared. Space was at a premium and the price of a berth skyrocketed.

Thousands of tons of supplies were arriving at the port cities and the streets began to look like giant warehouses. Merchants got rich selling anything connected with the Klondike and gold mining. The Canadian government required that each stampeder bring enough supplies with him to last one year. This averaged about 2,000 pounds and a cost of $500 in Seattle.

Many guide books were written suggesting what supplies should be taken. One such book listed the following items:

Flour	400 pounds
Bacon	150 pounds
Split Peas	150 pounds
Beans	100 pounds
Evaporated Apples	25 pounds
Evaporated Peaches	25 pounds
Apricots	25 pounds
Butter	25 pounds
Sugar	100 pounds
Condensed Milk	1 1/2 dozen cans
Coffee	15 pounds
Tea	10 pounds
Pepper	1 pound
Salt	10 pounds
Baking Powder	8 pounds
Rolled Oats	40 pounds
Yeast Cakes	2 dozen
4-oz. Beef Extract	1/2 dozen
Soap, Castile	5 bars
Soap, Tar	6 bars
Matches	1 tin
Vinegar	1 gallon
Candles	1 box
Evaporated Potatoes	25 pounds
Rice	25 pounds
Canvas Sacks	25 pounds
Wash Basin	1
Medicine Chest	1
Rubber Sheet	1
Pack Straps	1 set
Pick	1
Handle	1
Shovel	1
Gold Pan	1
Axe	1
Whip Saw	1
Hand Saw	1
Jack Plane	1
Brace	1
Bits, assorted	4
8" Mill File	1
6" Mill File	1
Broad Hatchet	1
2-Qt. Galvanized Coffee Pot	1
Fry Pan	1
Rivets	1 package
Draw Knife	1
Covered Pails	3
Pie Plate	1
Knife and Fork	1 each
Granite Cup	1
Tea and Table Spoon	1 each
14" Granite Spoon	1
Tape Measure	1
Chisel, 1 1/2"	1
Oakum	10 pounds
Pitch	10 pounds
20d Nails	5 pounds
10d Nails	5 pounds
6d Nails	6 pounds
5/8" Rope	200 feet
Single Block	1
Solder Outfit	1
14 Qt. Galvanized Pail	1
Granite Saucepan	1
Candlewick	3 pounds
Compass	1
Miner's Candlestick	1
Towels	6
Axe Handle	1
Axe Stone	1
Emery Stone	1
Sheet Iron Stove	1
Tent	1
Personal Clothes, extra Boots	
Sled for Winter Travel	

Many of the guide books placed the Klondike in Alaska, and few of the thousands of people who headed for the West Coast knew exactly where they were going.

The quickest route from the West Coast was up the Inside Passage Way of Canada and Alaska to the head of the Lynn Canal at Skagway, a journey of more than 1,000 miles. The Alaskan towns along the way enjoyed a boom of their own supplying the stampeders. Duties were placed on all goods brought into Canada from the United States and the British Columbia cities tried to capitalize on the fact that if an outfit was bought in Canada, no import duty would be placed on it. Duties on some items were: butter, 4 cents a pound; tobacco, 42 cents a pound; dogs and horses, 20 per cent; boots and shoes, 25 per cent; portable sawmills, 30 per cent. These were only minor details that stood in the way of the gold-crazed people. The rush was on and nothing could stop it.

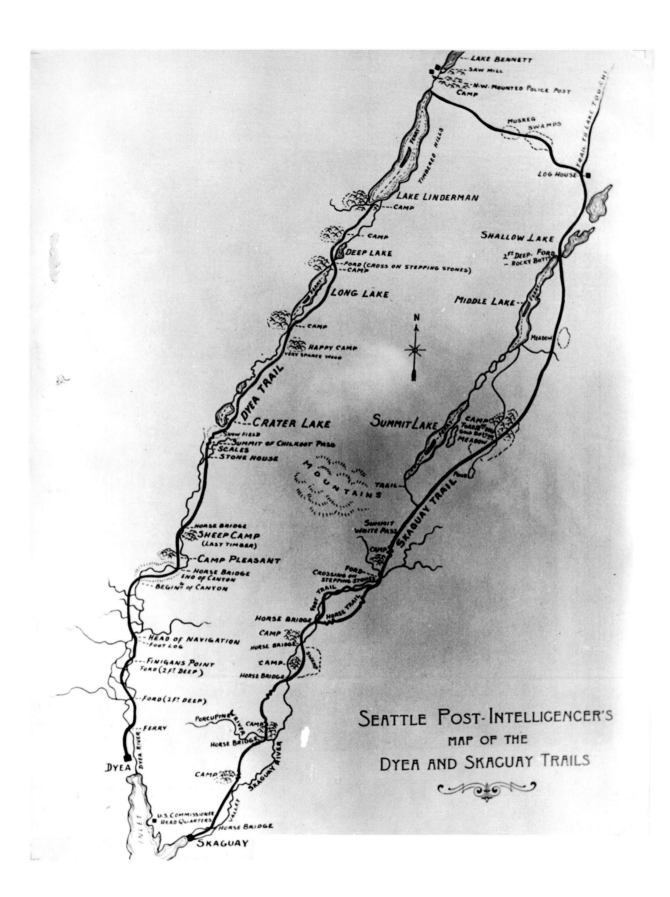

Map of the Dyea and Skagway Trails originally published in the *Seattle Post-Intelligencer* in 1897. The newspaper map made the trip look relatively easy. Then one started out on the trail, and things changed.

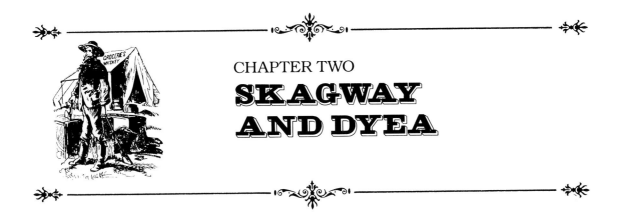

CHAPTER TWO

SKAGWAY AND DYEA

Captain William "Billy" Moore, the founder of Skagway, foresaw the gold rush many years before it actually happened. He staked a claim to 160 acres of land at the head of the Lynn Canal in 1887 and began building a pier on the tidal flats to bring in supplies. He had been a riverboat captain, packer, trader and prospector and was so knowledgeable in the ways of the North that William Ogilvie, the Canadian government surveyor, hired him to pack his party over the mountains into the interior and down the Yukon River. Moore decided to try a new route over the White Pass just north of the site of Skagway. Ogilvie's party went over the better-known Chilkoot Pass. The captain was enthusiastic about White Pass and had a vision of a large strike in the Yukon area, a railroad crossing White Pass and the town of Skagway providing the gateway. All of this was nine years before the actual gold rush occurred. Moore built a sawmill, worked to improve the site of the proposed town, and contracted for the mail route from Juneau to Fortymile and Circle City. This was quite a job for a man in his 70s. On one of his return trips to tidewater in 1896 he brought out news of the gold strike on Bonanza (Rabbit) Creek in August. Word was sent to Ottawa, but no action was taken by the Canadian government.

Things were to be quite different after the ships *Portland* and *Excelsior* brought word to the outside. The first horde of stampeders was in motion quickly.

The first shipload of prospectors unloaded at Skagway on July 26, 1897; immediately decided that Captain Moore had no right to the townsite, and promptly jumped his claim. His cabin was moved to its present site and a new town was laid out by Frank Reid, who anticipated the arrival of thousands of people. It took Moore four years of court battles to receive compensation for his original claim.

From the beginning, Skagway knew violence and lawlessness. Four companies of U.S. infantry were sent to Alaska during the height of the rush. Two companies each were attached to Dyea and Skagway. They settled disputes be-

Capt. William "Billy" Moore, the founder of Skagway and an early day developer of the Yukon country. AHL

Skagway, Alaska, at the head of the Lynn Canal in 1895. This was the starting point for the White Pass Trail to Lake Bennett. In two short years, the land that Captain Moore laid out as a town site would become a lawless boom town. UW 1895

Modern Skagway was once a major shipping terminus for goods moving to and from the Yukon and the southern terminus for the White Pass and Yukon Route. Today its main business is tourism.

With the Klondike strike, Skagway became a major gateway to the Yukon goldfields. In the summer of 1897, the first shiploads of prospectors from the Lower 48 began arriving at the town. Until large docks were built, the ships had to anchor offshore while small boats and lighters ferried men (and a few women) as well as goods and animals to the tidal flats.
TOP: AHL; MIDDLE: PABC

Supplies being unloaded in the Skagway harbor in 1897 before the docks were built. Barges brought the goods close to shore, and from there wagons hauled them over the tidal flats to the town. UW CURTIS 1897

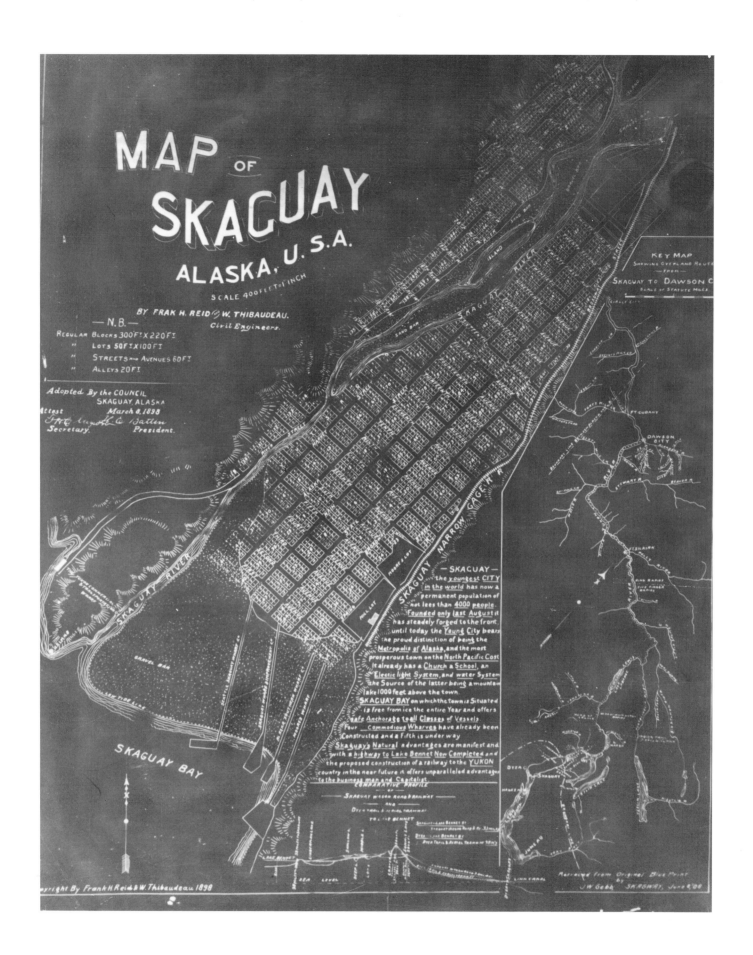

MAP OF SKAGUAY
ALASKA, U.S.A.

SCALE 400 FEET = 1 INCH

BY FRAK H. REID & W. THIBAUDEAU.
Civil Engineers.

— N.B. —
REGULAR BLOCKS 300 FT X 220 FT
" LOTS 50 FT X 100 FT
" STREETS and AVENUES 60 FT
" ALLEYS 20 FT

Adopted By the COUNCIL
SKAGUAY, ALASKA
Attest   March 8, 1898
Secretary.   President.

KEY MAP
SHOWING OVERLAND ROUTE
FROM
SKAGUAY TO DAWSON C

— SKAGUAY —
the youngest CITY in the world has now a permanent population of not less than 4000 people. Founded only last August it has steadily forged to the front, until today the Young City bears the proud distinction of being the Metropolis of Alaska, and the most prosperous town on the North Pacific Cost. It already has a Church, a School, an Electric light System, and water System the Source of the latter being a mountain lake 1000 feet above the town. SKAGUAY BAY on which the town is Situated is free from ice the entire Year and offers safe Anchorage to all Classes of Vessels. Four Commodious Wharves have already been Constructed and a Fifth is under way. Skaguay's Natural advantages are manifest and with a highway to Lake Bennet Now Completed and the proposed construction of a railway to the YUKON country in the near future it offers unparalleled advantages to the business man and Capitalist.

COMPARATIVE PROFILE
of
SKAGUAY WAGON ROAD & RAILWAY
and
DYE TRAIL & AERIAL TRAMWAY
TO LAKE BENNETT

Copyright By Frank H. Reid & W. Thibaudeau 1898

-22-

In 1892, Moore built this house, which would later be situated in the center of the intersection of Fifth and State streets. After much argument, he acquiesced to the town fathers' demands to move it, which was undertaken on Oct. 15, 1898. It no longer stands. The present fire department now occupies the site of the Jobbing house (extreme left).
YA BARLEY COLLECTION

Capt. William Moore stands in front of his original house, built in 1892 and decorated here for a Fourth of July celebration. He lived in a log cabin previous to 1892.
YA VANCOUVER PUBLIC LIBRARY COLLECTION

Captain Moore's original homestead cabin, built in 1887, now stands behind Kirmse's Jewelry Shop. It was moved 50 feet west to make room for an addition to the Ben Moore frame house, which was built in 1897-1899.
AUTHOR'S COLLECTION

Broadway Street in 1897, soon after the arrival of the first stampeders. The street would soon become a center of activity for the new gold-rush town. AHL

Broadway during its very early days. Compare this view, from June 1898, with later photos of the same street (pages 24 and 182). Looking north from Third Avenue.
MUSEUM OF HISTORY AND INDUSTRY, SEATTLE

Broadway Street today has lost its hustle and bustle, but still has the looks of 1898. The National Park Service has included part of Skagway in the Klondike Gold Rush National Historical Park.

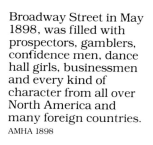

Broadway Street in May 1898, was filled with prospectors, gamblers, confidence men, dance hall girls, businessmen and every kind of character from all over North America and many foreign countries.
AMHA 1898

tween the Indians and the stampeders and guarded the Brackett Wagon Road. The Spanish-American War took some of the troops and commands were changed at various times until the early 1900s, when all the troops were withdrawn to the fort at Haines, Alaska. The troops were mostly ineffective in controlling the violence and con men in Skagway.

The need for a better trail from Skagway to White Pass was apparent early in the rush. A former mayor of Minneapolis, George Brackett, was hired by a hastily organized company to build a wagon road. He started construction in November 1897, but the promised funds never materialized and the supposed survey of the route was actually only a compass bearing. Even without funds, four miles were completed by late November and eight miles by mid-December. By then the company was broke and Brackett had to make a trip outside to raise money. He returned with enough to finish construction, and travelers started to use the toll road. The packers, however, refused to pay and troops had to be called in to maintain order. In April 1898, the East Fork of the Skagway River was bridged. This was one of the last major improvements on the road, which was used heavily until the railroad was completed to the summit of White Pass. The road never made money for Brackett or the company.

With Skagway booming from the influx of thousands of prospectors heading for Lake Bennett and the Klondike Gold Fields, there appeared on the scene Mr. Jefferson Randolph "Soapy" Smith. This lawless town was the perfect setting for Smith, who had learned his trade well as a con man in the mining camps of the American West. He gathered a gang of disreputable characters around him, and with them dominated the town and swindled many prospectors out of their money and supplies. Although he was out to fleece all prospectors passing through town, he rarely bothered the townspeople and was kind to women and children. He even raised a company of volunteers to fight in the Spanish-American War, a gesture the government turned down.

Lawlessness was soon to come to an end, however. A miner, J.D. Stewart, came to Skagway on July 7, 1898. His money was either lost or stolen—no one knows for sure—and he complained all over town. The long-inactive vigilante committee suspected Smith's gang and demanded that Stewart's money be returned.

Brackett's Trading Post later became the Skagway Home Power Building. AHL

Smith tried to force his way into a vigilantes' meeting at the Skagway wharf. In an encounter with one of the vigilantes, Frank Reid, shots were fired and both men fell to the deck of the wharf. Smith was dead. Reid, severely wounded, lived for 12 days. Both were buried in the cemetery north of Skagway. Smith's death was a relief to businessmen and stampeders, and Skagway returned to the business of catering to the thousands of people going north. Soapy Smith has remained one the best-known characters of the gold rush era.

From 15,000 at the height of the rush, Skagway's population had dropped to 600 by 1910. The decline in gold production in the 20th century and the depression of the 1930s almost ended Skagway's life as a town. World War II revived it, however, and today Skagway is a major tourist stop for tour boats and road travellers.

George Brackett, an ex-mayor of Minneapolis, constructed a wagon road part way up the White Pass Trail in the fall and winter of 1897-98. YA HEGG 1898

This road was the first real attempt to improve the route to the pass. It was a toll road and when the White Pass & Yukon Railway was formed, this road was included in the right-of-way. YA

Early view of Skagway when it had more tents than buildings. AHL

EARLY-DAY VIEWS OF SKAGWAY

When it opened in 1898, the Dewey ranked as one of the most fashionable hotels in town. Originally built at Seventh and State streets, it later was moved to a site across the street from the White Pass depot on the corner of Second and Broadway. The hotel burned down in 1940.
YA BARLEY COLLECTION

This unusual view shows one of Skagway's main streets in the early days. A few substantial buildings had been constructed by this time, but tents were still being used. This photo shows that Skagway was literally hacked out of the wilderness—the tree stumps in the middle of the street have not yet been uprooted.
YA MACBRIDE MUSEUM COLLECTION

The *Daily Alaskan* was an early Alaskan newspaper founded in February 1898. It continued publication under many different owners until 1924. YA BARLEY COLLECTION

An 1898 view of the four docks that were built out over Skagway's tidal flats. Constructing these docks was a massive undertaking. UW W&S 1898

Skagway's first drugstore, Kelly & Co. AHL

The Nome, located at the corner of Sixth and Broadway, was one of Skagway's most popular bars and gambling establishments. Built in 1899 and enlarged in 1900, it later became the Commerce Saloon. Today, it houses a restaurant and an inn. AHL

U.S. troops, of the 14th Infantry out of Vancouver Barracks, Wash., set up camp at Skagway in 1898. TRAIL OF 98 MUSEUM

A shipment of gold from the Klondike fields, brought down to Skagway by train, is displayed in front of the White Pass depot.
YA BARLEY COLLECTION

Moore's Wharf about 1900. In this view, mining machinery, cattle, and hay have been unloaded and await shipment by rail to the Yukon interior.
UAA, J.B. MOORE COLLECTION

The oldest frame building was formerly owned and occupied by Capt. Billy Moore. It later was the home of the Kirmse family and sits behind the Kirmse Jewelry Store.
UAA J.B. MOORE COLLECTION

The town was still bustling when this photo was taken in 1900, a year after the height of the gold rush was over. The town's main business would remain the transshipment of goods and materials to and from the Yukon.

1898. Dickey was a Presbyterian minister who spent six months in town before heading to the Klondike in April 1898. The church, which Dickey built, also served as a school and hospital.

Arrival of a dog team from far-away Dawson, Christmas 1898. Note the three hotels. The St. James and Brannick were two popular establishments. The St. James is still standing, on Fourth Avenue just east of Broadway. The Golden North Hotel, seen in the background, had not yet built its distinctive dome. This was not a white Christmas for Skagway.

The U.S. Courthouse, located just off Broadway on Seventh Avenue. The stone edifice, constructed in 1899 by the Methodist Church on a portion of Capt. Moore's homesite, originally housed McCabe College, Alaska's first institution of higher education. The building itself was Alaska's first granite structure. The school closed after only two terms of operation due to the passage of public school laws, and the building was sold to the federal government for use as a district court. In the 1950s, with the discontinuance of the court, the building was sold to the city of Skagway. Today it has been added on to and now houses City Hall and the Trail of 98 Museum. AHL

The Golden North at its present location on Broadway. By this time a third floor has been added. This building has been altered and it now houses a large gift shop. YA BARLEY COLLECTION

The Klondike Trading Co. built this two-story structure in 1898 on the corner of Third and State. From 1900 to 1904, the U.S. Army used it as a barracks, and in 1908 George Dedman and Edward Foreman bought the building, moved it to its present location on Broadway, added a third story and reopened it as the Golden North Hotel. Except for several years when it was closed due to financial problems, it has operated as a hotel ever since. This photo was taken about 1900 when the building stood on its original location and had only two stories. AHL

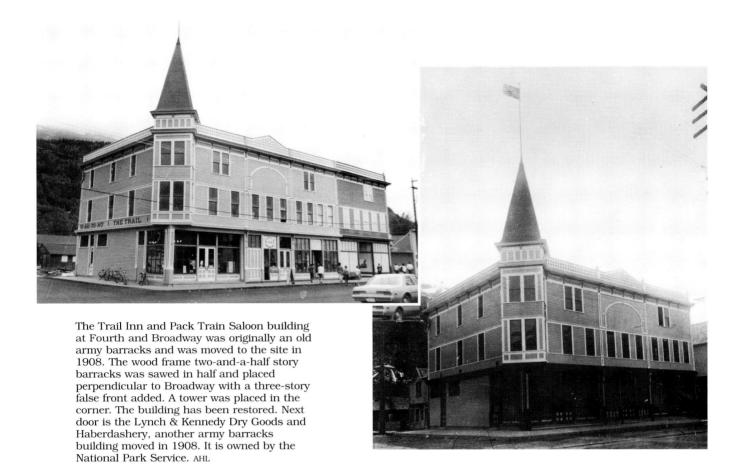

The Trail Inn and Pack Train Saloon building at Fourth and Broadway was originally an old army barracks and was moved to the site in 1908. The wood frame two-and-a-half story barracks was sawed in half and placed perpendicular to Broadway with a three-story false front added. A tower was placed in the corner. The building has been restored. Next door is the Lynch & Kennedy Dry Goods and Haberdashery, another army barracks building moved in 1908. It is owned by the National Park Service. AHL

Several buildings on Broadway's west side. The AB (Arctic Brotherhood) Hall was built in 1899 for the fraternal order. It has a facade of driftwood and sticks shaped into a mosaic of letters, gold pan and square patterns. President Warren G. Harding was the last initiated member of Camp Skagway No. 1 in 1923. It is now a visitors' center owned by the city of Skagway.

SKAGWAY SCENES TODAY

Richter's Jewelry & Curio Shop has occupied this building since the late 1920s. The right-side portion was built in 1899 and used as a ticket office and later a restaurant. The middle portion was built by J.H. Richter in 1929 and the left side in 1972.

The Mascot Saloon opened for business in 1898 and after Prohibition it became the Skagway Drug Store. Next door is the Pacific Clipper Line Office building, later to become part of the Mascot and drug store. Both buildings have been restored by the National Park Service.

This one-story frame structure was built in 1898 as a saloon but by 1901 it was the ticket office for the Pacific Coast Steamship Co. This lasted until the 1930s. It has been restored and now houses a gift shop.

The Eagle's Hall is made up of two 1898 hotels—the Mondamin and the Pacific, which were moved to the site between 1916-20. The facade was added in 1916. The Eagles acquired the building and remodeled it into a theater/hall. The "Days of 98" show is held here every summer.

Kirmse Jewelry Store was built in 1899 and remodeled for the jewelry store in 1904. Herman Kirmse opened his first Pioneer Jewelry Store in 1897 on Sixth Avenue. The north portion was acquired in 1906. Kirmse's son Jack operated the business until 1977 when it was sold. It is still in business today.

Dedman's Photo Shop occupies this 1897 building, which was E.A. Hegg's photo studio from 1897 to 1901. The building has been altered several times.

Dyea, at the end of Taiya Inlet, four miles from Skagway, enjoyed a boom of its own during the rush. It was on the route of the Chilkoot Trail and was built up rapidly after news of the gold strike reached the outside world. Since it could not accommodate ships as well as Skagway, it never achieved the size or status of its sister city.

The town grew quickly into a jumble of log and frame buildings, tents and a mass of humanity on the way to the Chilkoot Pass. It never had Skagway's stigma of violence because it was mainly a transient point on the trail, which remained open the year around.

With the completion of the railroad to Lake Bennett in 1899, Dyea and the Chilkoot Trail were abandoned. Today all that remains on the tidal flats are some posts that supported a pier and a few boards of former buildings. Such is the history of boom towns.

Until 1897, the only non-Indian structure at the site of Dyea was the Healy and Wilson Trading Post, established in 1885-86 by John J. Healy and Edgar Wilson. The post traded with local Indians until the great Klondike strike brought thousands of stampeders to the shores of Dyea, the starting point of the Chilkoot Trail which led to the Yukon's interior. AHL C.L. ANDREWS COLLECTION

Supplies are unloaded on the tidal flats of Dyea, Alaska, in 1898. Thousands of stampeders came through here in 1897-98 and tons of supplies were piled up on the beach waiting for transport up the Chilkoot Trail. YA VOGEE 1898

The main street of Dyea in 1898. It is typical of the towns that sprung up on the tidal flats and marshes—muddy streets and wood frame buildings, built one right next to another. But this was modern compared to the tent cities that were the beginnings of these towns. UW HEGG 1898

This is what Dyea looked like as the prospectors came up to it by boat in early 1897. Today a good gravel road connects it with Skagway, eight miles away.

All that remains of Dyea are some pier posts on the tidal flats and a few boards scattered around from former buildings. It is hard to imagine a city of thousands of people at this location.

Opposite: Like Skagway, Dyea sprang up almost overnight with the arrival of thousands of stampeders in 1897-98.
AHL

Above: By March, 1899, less than two years after the arrival of the first stampeders, Dyea's future was looking bleak. The White Pass and Yukon Route railroad was inching its way from Skagway toward Lake Bennett and would soon eliminate the need for the Chilkoot Trail. Without the Chilkoot Trail, Dyea had no reason to exist.
YA VOGEE COLLECTION

DYEA ALASKA MARCH 1899   COPYRIGHT 1899   VOGEE

Cemetery for victims of the snow slide at the bottom of the Chilkoot Pass on April 3, 1898. Sixty-three men died under tons of snow, but the avalanche did not stop the flow of stampeders up the pass. The cemetery is one mile from the Dyea townsite near the beginning of the Chilkoot Trail.

A few building remains and artifacts could still be seen in the 1980s. The area is now part of the Klondike Gold Rush National Historical Park with interpretive signs, a campground and trailhead for the Chilkoot Trail.

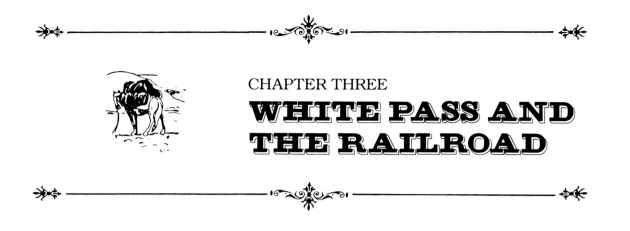
The White Pass or Skagway Trail wandered 45 miles from Skagway to Lake Bennett and was one of the two passes that opened up the interior of the Yukon. It had been named by William Ogilvie, the Canadian government surveyor, after Thomas White, the Canadian Minister of the Interior.

Although it was lower in elevation than Chilkoot Pass and stock animals could be used to pack supplies, the trail turned into a nightmare of death and horror for those who used it. The route crossed swamps, bogs, high mountains, deep canyons, dense forests and areas of large boulders. Hundreds of streams and creeks had to be crossed, many flooding after heavy rains. With the thousands of pack animals and prospectors tramping down the trail it soon became deeply rutted and muddy and was difficult for animals to walk over. It was so narrow that two animals had trouble passing each other.

At times, because of flooding, snowslides or dead animals, the trail became blocked for days and people and animals were backed up clear to Skagway.

Nothing was more pitiful than the plight of the horses used to pack supplies over the trail to Lake Bennett. Many were in bad shape before being brought to the trail from the West Coast, and the packers had no idea how to handle them. Their only concern was to get to Lake Bennett the fastest way possible.

Most of the 3,000 animals used on the trail died in Dead Horse Canyon, and the heaps of carcasses left travelers with a sight they never forgot.

It is no wonder that the Chilkoot Trail was more popular with the stampeders.

The early dream of Captain Moore for a railroad crossing the mountains was about to come true. A meeting in Skagway between Sir Thomas Tanerede, representing a group of British investors, and Mike Heney, a railroad contractor, resulted in the formation of the White Pass and Yukon Railroad Company in April 1898. Serious doubts were raised as to the feasibility of building a railroad through the steep mountains, but Heney insisted he could do it.

Construction began on May 27, 1898. Brackett's Wagon Road was bought out, as the road would be put out of business upon completion of the railroad. Part of the route of the railroad follows the old wagon road.

596. LOOKING UP WHITE PASS SUMMIT FROM HALF MILE BELOW MAR. 20-99.

Winter travel on the White Pass Trail was rough. Although freight could be sledded, there was no feed or water for the animals. Snow obscured the trail and ice was hard on man and beasts.
UW HEGG 1899

Hauling 1,400 pounds with one horse over White Pass summit.
UW HEGG

Sometimes whole families went over the passes using whatever hauling conveyance they could find.
AUTHOR'S COLLECTION

Packers on the White Pass Trail (also called the Skagway Trail) used anything that would pull a load-horses, dogs, oxen, goats and mules. The trail was a series of bogs, swamps and mountains. In most places it was not wide enough for two animals to pass. Porcupine Hill, shown at top photo, was a mass of boulders and hard for horses to walk through.
TOP: AHL GOETZMAN; BOTTOM: UW HEGG

Transporting the ton of supplies needed by each stampeder was a monumental task, and every means was used. Usually people banded together to get supplies over the pass. Horses, dogs, goats, and mules were used for hauling. Although both passes were rugged, the White Pass lent itself more to animal power than the Chilkoot Pass.

TOP: BETTMANN ARCHIVE/NEW YORK BOTTOM:UW LA ROUCHE 1897

The original "Trail of 98."

Of the 3,000 horses that were used to pack over the pass, only a handful survived. The others died in what became known as Dead Horse Canyon, from cruel treatment, neglect and overloading. The demand for horses was so great in Seattle that anything that could stand up was sent north.
UW CURTIS

THE DEAD HORSE TRAIL.

The Dead Horse Trail.
AMHA

Dead Horse Canyon as seen from the tracks of the White Pass and Yukon Railroad. Little had changed in 80 years.

Looking down through cut-off canyon from a half-mile below the White Pass Summit, March 1899. UW

The summit of White Pass, winter 1898.
AMHA, HEGG 1898

SUMMIT OF WHITE PASS.

PACK TRAINS ON THE SUMMIT OF WHITE PASS. COPYRIGHT 1898.

View of White Pass City just a few miles out of Skagway on the White Pass Trail. A small cluster of tents and wooden buildings were built here to service the stampeders coming and going on the trail. The town disappeared when the railroad crossed over the pass and reached Lake Bennett in 1899. AMHA CASE & DRAPER

To save construction costs a three-foot narrow-gauge line was decided on. This reduced the roadbed from 15 feet to 10 feet, an important factor in this mountainous terrain.

The track reached the summit of White Pass on February 18, 1899, but was stopped by the Canadian authorities at the international border. It took some persuasion, a bottle of scotch and a little trickery before work could proceed past the border. The tracks were completed to Lake Bennett on July 6, 1899.

The only tools the workers had were picks, shovels and blasting powder. The construction continued all through the winter months with high winds, cold and blizzards making work extremely difficult. Many of the workers stayed only long enough to earn a grubstake and then joined the endless procession of stampeders heading for Dawson or the new gold discovery at Atlin, British Columbia.

Construction had also started from the northern terminus at Whitehorse, and the tracks met at Carcross, Yukon Territory, on July 29, 1900. With the completion of the route (at a cost of about $10,000,000) the mountains were no longer a barrier to people wishing to enter the interior of the Yukon. The railroad also operated river boats to Dawson in the summer and a stage line in the winter.

In 21 miles to the summit, the railroad climbs 2,885 feet with an average grade of 2.6 percent. It consists of 20 miles in Alaska, 32 miles in British Columbia and 58 miles in the Yukon for a total of 110 miles.

With the decline in gold production in mid-century, the railroad came upon hard times. During World War II the U.S. Army took it over and the line served a vital role in hauling supplies for the construction of the Alaska Highway. In 1982 economic conditions and the closing of mining activity in the Yukon forced the railroad to close.

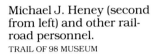
Michael J. Heney (second from left) and other railroad personnel.
TRAIL OF 98 MUSEUM

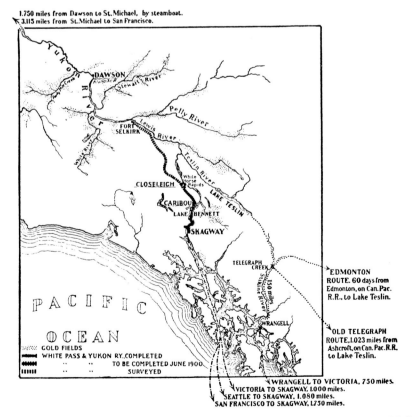

MAP OF THE WHITE PASS AND YUKON RAILWAY, SHOWING THE PART ALREADY COMPLETED, THE PART NOW UNDER CONSTRUCTION, AND THE PART SURVEYED FOR FUTURE CONSTRUCTION.

Temporary Skagway quarters in 1898 for the White Pass railway.
YA BARLEY COLLECTION

Clearing Broadway for placement of railroad tracks, spring 1898. The town still had a frontier character. UW

Laying rails along the bluff in Skagway, 1898. Most of these workers probably would scatter to the next gold strike in the Yukon, British Columbia, or Alaska.
YA BARLEY COLLECTION

Top left: A wooden hoist lifts heavy boulders. Many improvised methods were used to lighten the work. YA BARLEY

Top right: Railway workers used ropes to support themselves as they cut the railway grade on a steep face of Tunnel Mountain in September 1898. YA BARLEY

This was the only tunnel on the route. Thousands of tons of rock had to be blasted, then dug and moved out by hand. UW HEGG 1898

Members of F. B. Flood's engineering corps pose with surveying instruments in front of their tent in September 1898. YA BARLEY

Removing the rubble after blasting was back-breaking work. Thousands of men toiled with pick and shovel to cut the roadbed from solid rock. YA BARLEY

Construction workers use sledge hammers to pound a steel rod into rock to make a hole for a blasting charge. YA BARLEY

Hand labor at the end of the grade near the summit on August 25, 1898. YA BARLEY

The first passenger train to the summit enters the tunnel on February 20, 1899. UW HEGG

The steel cantilever bridge as it appears to-day. It was abandoned in 1969 when the new shorter bridge and tunnel were completed.

STEEL ARCH BRIDGE
JUNE 10, 1901

The steel arch bridge spanning Dead Horse Canyon. The bridge was built in 1901 and was the highest steel cantilever bridge in the world when built. A roundhouse sits on the wooden trestle. Before the bridge was completed a switchback was used to negotiate the deep gorge. Trains went up the gorge and then had to back uphill to reach the summit.
YA

Station at the summit of White Pass. YA BARLEY

The summit of White Pass. Here the stampeders who were lucky enough to make it met the Mounted Police and customs officials. This view shows the border and the railroad, with Summit Lake in the background. UW HEGG

Summit Lake today shows little effect from the mass of stampeders in 1897-99.
COURTESY WHITE PASS AND YUKON RAILROAD

A White Pass excursion train crosses the small timber trestle at Rocky Point in May 1900. YA

The entire 110-mile railroad was completed on July 29, 1900, 26 months after construction began and at an expenditure of about $10,000,000. The last spike was driven at Carcross, and the long grueling trip over the passes and down to Whitehorse was a thing of the past.
YA BARLEY 1900

WHITE PASS AND YUKON ROUTE   43

Pass one person from Skaguay to White Pass Summit and Return, February 20th, 1899, when stamped with Company stamp, to witness ceremonies connected with the completion of the tracks to Summit of White Pass.

E. C. HAWKINS,   L. H. GRAY,
         General Supt.,   Gen. Traffic Mngr.
         Skaguay, Alaska.   Skaguay, Alaska.

Driving the last spike at Lake Bennett on July 6, 1899. The mountain barrier had at last been spanned by steel rails. UW W & S

The railroad was completed to Lake Bennett, a distance of 40 miles, on July 6, 1899. A train left that day for Skagway carrying a fortune in gold from the Klondike. It had taken a little over a year to reach this point from Skagway. UW HEGG 1899

The original railroad bridge at Carcross, looking north.

The Carcross Station, built in 1902 and enlarged in 1925. The golden spike ceremony marking the completion of the railroad was held here on July 29, 1900. It is now a visitors' center.

Reminders of the past at Carcross. The *Duchess* was first build as a 2'6" gauge engine and widened to the 3-foot gauge when sold to the White Pass in 1899. Retired in 1910.

Tracks of the White Pass & Yukon Route, since 1988 a tourist railroad.

The last original building on the railroad at Fraser faces the new Canadian customs building across the Carcross-Skagway road. The old building was a water tank for locomotives and rotary snowplows. A turn-a-round was provided there for the equipment. sc

The Caribou Hotel at Carcross. With the abandonment of the railroad in 1982, the Carcross-Skagway Highway is the only land link to interior Yukon from tidewater. Carcross has become a large tourist mecca for visitors to the North Country.

The first locomotive on the railroad was bought in 1898 after it had seen long service on the Utah and Northern Railroad. It was built in 1881 and remained in service on the railroad until 1940. PABC

The first locomotive used on the railroad was renumbered #52 after modification in 1900. It was on display in Skagway for years.

Exterior of the White-horse depot, facing the waterfront in 1901. YA

The White Pass and Yukon Route station at the north end of Main Street in Whitehorse. It was built in 1900 and remodeled in 1953. It is now used as office space and ticket office for the railroad.

The stately railroad administration building and depot, now the home of the National Park Service's visitor center in Skagway. YA BARLEY

Engine Number 7 picking up passengers at the Skagway depot, early 1900s. UW

Hotel hacks at the depot, early 1900s. YA BARLEY

A rotary clears the rails in the early 1900s. PABC

Rotary snowplow No. 1 on display in Skagway. The rotaries were replaced in the 1950s by bulldozers to clear the tons of snow on the rails.

Some original passenger cars on the siding at Skagway. They are used for the tourist railroad running daily in summer to the summit.

A White Pass train arriving at Skagway in the early 1900s. YA CALLARMAN

Log Cabin, British Columbia, was just over the summit of White and Chilkoot passes. The Canadian customs office was located here, and it was a welcome stop after the grueling trip over the pass. UW HEGG

Top: Customs House at Log Cabin, first major stop on the railroad after crossing the White Pass. Bottom: Headquarters of the North West Mounted Police at Log Cabin. The police were stationed all along the trail from the top of the passes to Dawson to maintain law and order. YA

CHAPTER FOUR
CHILKOOT TRAIL AND LAKE BENNETT

Of the many familiar scenes of the gold rush era, one stands out as the symbol of the Klondike—the climb to the Chilkoot Pass. Although the pass is more than 500 miles from the gold fields, it has been impressed on people's minds as the sum of all the hardships of the trip and of the whole crazy period.

The Chilkoot Trail began at Dyea and extended for 33 miles to Lake Bennett, the head of navigation for the Yukon River system. The trail had been used for years by the Chilkat Indians to cross the mountains and by early prospectors traveling to the Yukon interior.

Today the trail follows most of the original route to Lake Lindeman. It starts one mile from the Dyea townsite at the south end of the Taiya River bridge and extends for 33 miles to Lake Bennett. (The first 14 miles consist of a series of steep ascents interspersed with level walking through dense growth, over streams and along an old logging road.) From the base of the pass the trail traverses six miles of perpetual snow fields and rock above timberline. It then dips and climbs the rest of the way to Lake Lindeman at Mile 26. The last seven miles to Lake Bennett do not follow an early trail since the stampeders used boats to get between the lakes.

John J. Healy and Edgar Wilson had established a trading post at the tidewater site of Dyea in 1886 to trade with Indians and to supply prospectors crossing the pass on their way to the gold strikes at Fortymile and Circle. They were in a good position for the horde of people that came in 1897.

The Chilkoot Pass has an elevation of 3,739 feet. More people chose this route rather than the White Pass, because Chilkoot was open all year and its trail to Lake Bennett was shorter by a few miles. An estimated 20,000 to 30,000 people tra-

veled the trail in 1897-98. It was the experience of a lifetime.

The Canadian government saw early in the rush that people heading for the Yukon would have to take care of themselves for a long time. It required everyone to bring about a ton of supplies—enough to last a year. (A tariff was imposed on these supplies if they had been bought in the United States.) This strict rule undoubtedly saved many lives.

Chilkat Indians were employed to transport goods up the Chilkoot Pass for so much per pound.

Actresses fording the Taiya River on the way to promised jobs in Dawson. One "lady" is getting some help. One wonders where their supplies are and who is packing them over the trail. UW LaROCHE 1897

Transporting the ton of supplies needed by each stampeder was a monumental task, and every means was used. Usually people banded together to get supplies over the pass. Horses, dogs, goats, mules, and the local Indians were used. Although both passes were rugged, the White Pass lent itself more to animal power than the Chilkoot Pass. UW LaRoche 1897

A surgeon's tent on the trail. It is amazing that there were not more deaths and injuries during the two year gold rush considering the number of people not used to harsh conditions and rugged terrain.
BETTMANN ARCHIVE/NEW YORK

Packers resting on the trail. A tablecloth has been spread between poles as a shield against the summer sun and rain. UW LaROCHE 1897

After miles of trail, fresh pie, doughnuts and coffee must have been too great a temptation for the weary traveler to pass up. It is hard to tell just where the pastries were baked. The prices were not bad, though, by today's standards. UW CURTIS 1898

With close to 2,000 pounds of supplies to haul, the prospectors found that local Indians provided a much-needed service. The Indians could pack enormous loads, and charged 12 cents a pound for packing from Dyea to the Scales at the base of the pass. When the demand for packers increased, the price went up. Some charged $1 a pound over the pass. Even with the packers available, most stampeders could not afford the charge and ended up hauling their own supplies over the trail.

Incredible stories have been told of the type of supplies hauled over the trail. One man supposedly hauled a piano on his back, and a steamboat was reportedly taken over piece by piece. Many women traveled the trail, a few in fancy dresses. Some children made the trip.

The force that drove them on was the desire to get to the gold fields before anyone else. As it turned out, no matter how fast they made it over the pass in the fall and winter of 1897-98, they were stuck at Lakes Lindeman and Bennett until the spring breakup. It took the average stampeder three months or more to haul his supplies over the trail.

All along the trail enterprising people set up hotels and lunch counters and provided other services. Many became rich before they ever reached the gold fields. Several towns were established along the trail to provide rest stops and supplies.

Left: Parts of the Chilkoot Trail were through marshy and boggy ground, so corduroy roads were put in to make the walking easier. The trail for the tramway can be seen along with one of the tripods for the cable. The man in the foreground has some horsepower to make his trip easier.
YA LANE 1898

Right: A portion of the corduroy road as it appears today on the trail above Sheep Camp. Most of the trail up to timberline is overgrown and it would be difficult to keep on it without the maintenance work done by the National Park Service.

The people who set up hotels, restaurants and other types of businesses along the trail made more money than most of the prospectors heading for the Klondike. Most of these establishments were simple tents with a minimum of equipment and provisions. The hotels simply provided a place for a man to lay down his blankets. A telegraph line was set up in February, 1898, and provided communications with tidewater and eventually the outside world. COURTESY RICHARD MOLL, FREEPORT, ILLINOIS

Part of the original trail as it looks today. The trail is now maintained by Parks Canada and the U.S. National Park Service. It follows the original trail most of the way to Lake Lindeman.

Some artifacts left along the trail between Deep Lake and Lake Lindeman. Frying pans were among the items most often abandoned by the weary stampeders.

One of the original telegraph poles still standing along the trail. The crossarms are intact. Many miles of wire can still be found along the trail. When the line reached above the timberline, metal poles had to be placed in the rocks to withstand the pressures of the deep snow.

Crime was not a great problem on the trail because everyone was intent on getting his own supplies through, and there were few places for a criminal to hide. Trail justice was swift for those who did get caught, however, and this chap appears about to be strapped to a tripod pole and be lashed. He was probably sent back down to Dyea and forbidden to push on to his goal of Dawson. YA

Remains of a steam boiler at the Canyon City townsite. This possibly was used to produce electric lighting in several camps along the trail.

Building and artifacts at the Canyon City townsite. The building could be part of the tramway complex. It is hard to picture a sizable community at this overgrown site, but 20 wooden structures were built in the area, including restaurants, hotels, bars and stores.

The Chilkoot Railroad and Transportation Company's tramway in operation between Canyon City and Crater Lake, a distance of 8 miles. This tramway was opened in May 1898 to haul freight over the pass. Tripods were built up the trail and an endless cable was suspended between with buckets attached to haul the freight. Although it broke down frequently, the tram served its purpose until the White Pass Railroad was completed to Lake Bennett. Freight was hauled at 7 1/2 cents a pound. The tram had a bad effect on the Indians who made a living packing on the trail. UW HEGG 1898

-72-

A portion of Sheep Camp, named for the hunters who used the area as a headquarters for sheep hunting before the rush. This was the last large settlement before the summit and Lake Lindeman. As the structures were wedged in between the mountain and the Taiya River, Sheep Camp was susceptible to floods in the spring of 1898. Here goods of any description could be bought and it was a starting point for the packers going up to the summit. UW CURTIS

Artifacts at the Sheep Camp site. This area is so overgrown that it is hard to imagine a settlement here in the past. The final rest shelter before the trip over the pass to Lake Lindeman is located here.

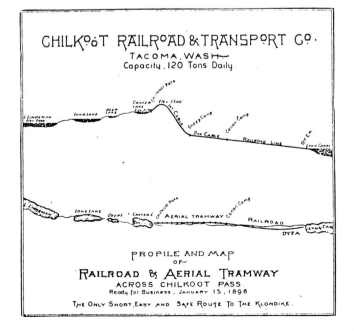

CHILKOOT RAILROAD & TRANSPORT CO.
TACOMA, WASH.
Capacity, 120 Tons Daily.

PROFILE AND MAP
OF
RAILROAD & AERIAL TRAMWAY
ACROSS CHILKOOT PASS.
Ready for Business, JANUARY 15, 1898.

THE ONLY SHORT, EASY AND SAFE ROUTE TO THE KLONDIKE.

Canyon City, built along the Taiya River eight miles from Dyea, was the starting point for the tramway across the summit. It was mainly a tent town, but provided needed services. Farther along the trail, Sheep Camp was established, so named because sheep hunters had camped there in the past. This was the last major stop before the summit, and travelers could get a bunk and a meal. In September 1898, an ice dam holding back water in one of the high glaciers broke and a wall of water 20 feet high swept through the town. Only one man drowned but most of the tents were swept away.

Once the gold stampede began in earnest, men began to construct all sorts of systems for getting supplies and paraphernalia over the pass. Archie Burns built the first hoist using a gasoline engine, and a pulley drum to haul up a sled by cable. Several others built primitive aerial tramways. By far the most elaborate was the Chilkoot Railroad and Transportation Company's. It ran from Canyon City, over the pass, and down to Crater Lake, a distance of eight miles.

This tramway was professionally engineered with a series of tripods and constructed up the trail with cable strung between them. Loads up to 400 pounds could be carried at one time for a fee of 7-1/2 cents per pound. The tram opened in May 1898 and put a lot of the Indian packers out of business.

Even with the tram in operation, many stampeders continued to haul their own supplies. Some used horses in summer and sleds in winter to get to the Scales. From there the traveler reached the summit by going up 1,200 steps cut in the ice. All through the winter of 1897-98, thousands of people in an endless line trudged up these "Golden Stairs." If one stepped out of line to rest, it took him hours to regain a spot. Each person had to repeat the trip as many as 30 times before he had all his supplies at the summit and cached. The trip back to the Scales to pick up the next load was simpler. The traveler slid down on a shovel or piece of tin or on his back. Many people arriving at the Scales and seeing the long line and steep climb sold their outfits or abandoned them and returned to Dyea and the outside world. The entire trail became a gigantic junkyard as people shed what they thought were unnecessary items.

There was chaos at the summit. As only about 70 pounds could be carried up the pass at one time, the stampeder had to mark a spot for his

A view of Long Hill looking south near the start up the steep summit climb from Sheep Camp. For the stock animals on this portion of the trail it must have been very hard, with harsh weather conditions and heavy loads. UW HEGG 1898

The same scene today. Weather conditions are unpredictable in this country and one has to be prepared for any type of storm, from rain and high winds to snow.

The tramway hauls a boat to the summit. Although this was an easy method for getting supplies to the summit, most of the prospectors could not afford the steep freight rate and had to pack close to 2,000 pounds of supplies to the top themselves.
UW HEGG 1898

Remains of a tramway tripod and building thought to have been a restaurant and tramway office just below the Scales. The trail now is above timberline.

cache. In the winter, with blizzards raging frequently, he rammed a long pole into the snow next to his supplies so he could find them. With thousands of people hauling up supplies, space on the summit was limited.

The North West Mounted Police established the border at the summit, checked everyone for the required supplies and collected tariffs on them. Weather conditions were intolerable that winter and both police and stampeders suffered horribly. Up to 70 feet of snow fell and it was hard to keep men, goods and tents on top of it.

April 1898 brought a major disaster. A heavy storm a few days before had deposited deep soft snow on the pass. Then it warmed up for a few days. These were perfect conditions for the avalanche that occurred on April 3. Sixty-three people were buried. After the bodies were dug out and hauled back down the trail, the endless procession resumed.

When a complete outfit had reached the summit it was hauled in relays to Crater Lake and then by sled or horses to either Lake Lindeman or Lake Bennett. The relay of supplies along the trail ballooned the 34-mile hike to upwards of 2,000 miles.

Tramway cable wire can still be seen along the trail.

Modern-day hikers climb to the summit in the summer. Even then there are many snowfields to cross.

The scramble to the summit in the summer. It was actually easier to reach the pass in the winter because the giant boulders pictured were hard to climb with a heavy pack. For the average hiker today a 40-pound pack is a good load and frequent rest stops are needed. UW L & D

UW

View of the trail below the Scales and some of the Chilkat Indian packers resting before ascending to the summit. In the summer the trail was cut through the rocks, although perpetual snowfields were found along the way. The top view was taken before the long tramway was built and the bottom view shows the same area today. The trail along here is marked by cairns and flags up to the summit. UW

LaROUCHE 1897

Close-up of the Scales and the climb up the "Golden Stairs." The Scales were used to weigh the packs before they were transported to the summit by the Indians or the various tramways in operation. FROM A STEREOSCOPE VIEW 1897

When one thinks of the Klondike Gold Rush this picture of the trail to Chilkoot Pass probably comes to mind. It is the most-publicized view of the entire 600-mile trip from tidewater down the Yukon to Dawson. The main route, but the steeper one, is to the left, where there was a continuous line of people day and night all the way back to Sheep Camp. A lower but longer trail, the Peterson Trail, is to the right. It was used mainly by horses and dog teams. The Scales are shown in the middle. UW HEGG 1898

On Palm Sunday, April 3, 1898, a snowslide occurred on the right of the pass, killing 63 men. The bodies were dug out and taken down to Sheep Camp. Even this event did not stop the mad scramble for the summit.

UW HEGG 1898

An endless string of men climbs the "Golden Stairs," steps chipped in the ice with a rope strung along the way for guidance. 1,200 steps were cut up a 30-degree slope for a total vertical climb of 500 feet. In a two-year period up to 30,000 men and women and even some children walked over the trail. Countless numbers reached the bottom of the summit, saw the grueling climb and abandoned their equipment and returned to Dyea.

UW HEGG 1898

Packing Up Chilkoot Pass

PASS.   COPYRIGHT 1898.   E. Hegg.

On Chilkoot Pass

The average stampeder took an hour to make the climb with a pack load of 70 pounds. An Indian packer could carry 100 pounds and some are reported to have carried incredible burdens in the hundreds of pounds. If a man got off the trail for any reason it sometimes took him hours to get back in line, so steady was the procession and so much in a hurry were the stampeders to get to the top. Once at the top the packer returned by the quickest means, either sliding to the bottom on a shovel or on his back. It could take a stampeder up to 30 trips to the summit to get his required ton of supplies assembled in one place. UW CANTWELL

The trail now follows marked poles up the left side of the picture and is best climbed on all fours.

A series of
photos taken at
the bottom of
the steep climb
to the summit.

Canadian police check stampeders at the summit. UW CURTIS

The author and his wife at the summit of the pass and the international border. The author is holding a leather boot found along the trail. The plaque in the middle is one of a series placed along the trail to tell its story.

Once at the summit the stampeder cached his supplies and went down for the next load. With 70 feet of snow that winter, he had to stick poles by his cache to find it again. Some supplies were not dug out until spring. The police checked every man, collected the appropriate duty and advised him of conditions along the trail. An attempt was made to weed out the loafer, criminal or ill-prepared and send him back to Dyea. Everyone had to be prepared for the worst the Yukon could throw at him. YA

Canadian
customs at the
summit of the
pass.

Typical weather
conditions in the
winter of 1897-
98 at the sum-
mit. With snow-
storms like this,
strong winds
and tempera-
tures down to
50° below it is a
wonder that
anyone sur-
vived. The flag is
flying at the
Canadian cus-
toms house.

Customs house at the summit. The North West Mounted Police established the summit as the international boundary early in the rush and, fearful that many people would come into Canada ill-prepared, required at least one ton of supplies (to last a year) for each person entering the country. They were also there to help the stampeders and of course to collect duty on the supplies brought across the border. YA PRATHER

Remains of the customs house and NWMP station at the international border. The building was not much for comfort and the Mounties must have suffered as much as the stampeders in the winter of 1897-98.

The tramway cable went up to the summit and then down the other side to Crater Lake where it was anchored by the large crib filled with stones. The freight was then taken down to Long Lake for the haul to Lake Bennett. UW HEGG 1899

Remains of the stone crib just below the summit on Crater Lake.

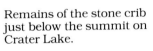

Artifacts at the summit of the pass.

Freight at Long Lake. Part of this freight probably came up on the tramway to be packed on horses for the five-mile trip to Lake Lindeman.
YA 1898

View of Long Lake from the trail above it.

An abandoned boat on the shore of Crater Lake was probably used for ferrying freight across the lake. From Crater Lake it was another nine miles to Lake Lindeman and the first camp for boat building.

The White Pass and Chilkoot trails both ended at Lake Bennett in British Columbia. From there it was a 550-mile float trip down the Yukon River to Dawson.

All through the summer and fall of 1897 and the winter of 1898 thousands of stampeders crossed the passes to the lakes and began the long process of building boats to float the river. Those who reached the lakes before freeze up could leave immediately if they had packed boats with them, but most were held up at the lakes until the spring breakup.

The town at Lake Bennett became the largest tent city in the world. By the spring of 1898 it had a population of more than 10,000. Its residents were camped all along the shores of the lake and back up along the rapids toward Lake Lindeman. The forests for miles around had been cleared to provide the lumber necessary to build thousands of boats. Vessels of every description were under construction, although most of the people had never built a boat before. Some were to find out on their journey downriver that they should have paid more attention to the construction.

The delay at Bennett, waiting for the spring breakup, must have been unbearable. The treasure lay only 550 miles downriver, but the stampeders could not reach it. If they had known that most of the streams had already been staked they might have had second thoughts about continuing.

The police moved among the boat builders giving advice and settling disputes. Lumber for the boats was provided by a back-breaking device called a whipsaw. This consisted of an open scaffold on which a log was placed. Planks were cut from the log with a long two-handled saw, one man sawing from below and the other from above. This primitive technique was the cause of more partnership breakups than any other single thing. It was not uncommon for two men to split up their outfits. In a few instances they even cut their boats in two.

On May 28, 1898, the ice began to break up and by the 29th, boats could navigate the lake. That day more than 7,000 boats of every description started down the lake. One could almost walk across the lake without touching water. Bennett was virtually deserted overnight. It would never be the same again.

Lake Lindeman and Lindeman City in the summer of 1898. This was the end of the land journey for many stampeders who stopped here to build boats for the trip down the Yukon. Thousands of tents were pitched along the shores. YA HEGG 1898

Lake Lindeman is now mostly overgrown but many artifacts can still be found among the trees. The overnight shelters have been built here by the Canadian government to accommodate hikers on the trail.

Artifacts on the flats of the old townsite of Lindeman City.

The cemetery on the hill above Lake Lindeman contains the remains of stampeders who died along the trail. With the incredible hardships along the trail, some died of the cold, some of sickness and accidents and a few by their own hand.

The rapids between Lakes Lindeman and Bennett forced the stampeders to portage supplies and carefully maneuver boats with ropes. The NWMP tents are in the background.
UW LaROCHE 1897

Little has changed in this scene since 1897.

This was Bennett, the largest tent city in the world and the end of the hike from tidewater. More than 10,000 people camped here in the winter of 1897-98, building boats and waiting for the ice to break for the trip down the Yukon to Dawson.
AHL GOETZMAN 1898

Dock remains at Lake Bennett.

Views of boat building on Lake Bennett. Most of the trees for miles around the lake had been cut down to saw into lumber for boats, buildings and firewood. Boats of every description were built for a flotilla that would also include portable canoes and kayaks brought over the trails. Work went on night and day so that all would be ready for the spring breakup and the final trip down the Yukon to Dawson 550 miles away. UW

Building a boat at Windy Arm on Lake Bennett in the winter of 1897-98. Most of the stampeders who made it to Bennett had no idea how to build a boat but, necessity being the mother of invention, they soon learned the rudiments of the skill. Everything but the lumber for the boats—the nails, caulking, sails—had to be carried over the Chilkoot Pass. Usually a group of men got together to construct one boat big enough for all the men and their supplies. UW CURTIS

ON THE

1. Whip-sawing Lumber.   2. Har

KLONDIKE—BOAT-BUILDING AT LAKE LINDEMAN.—From Photographs by Tappan Adney, Special Correspondent of "Harper's Weekly."—[See Page 19.]

ards.   3. Spar-making.   4. Boat under Construction.   5. Tappan Adney and his Dory.   6. Calking the Seams.   7. Finishing Touches.   8. His Dory and Tappan Adney.   9. A Launching-Bee.

Harper's Weekly,
January 1, 1898. AMHA

This device broke up more partnerships than anything else. It is a whipsaw or "arm-strong," used for sawing boards for buildings and boats. The sawyer on the bottom got a shower of sawdust, and tempers grew short when one partner accused the other of not doing his share. Later, sawmills were set up to fill the demands for lumber.
YA VOGEE 1898

By 1899 the gold rush was over and a traveler could ride the railroad to Lake Bennett and then take a river boat down the Yukon. By the time the railroad reached Whitehorse in June 1900, Bennett was no longer important other than as a stop on the railroad. UW BARLEY 1899

Lake Bennett about 1900. UW

Today Lake Bennett is one of the most beautiful of the Yukon lakes and, until 1982, a major tourist stop on the railroad. The railroad station was built after 1900 and would be just to the right of center in the top picture.

Lake Bennett looking north from the unfinished church built on its shore in 1898. This building is the only one remaining from the gold rush days. A cemetery is just above the church. This was the end of the Chilkoot and White Pass trails, a 30- to 40-mile trip from tidewater Alaska.

The day after the ice broke up on Lake Bennett on May 29, 1898, more than 7,000 boats took off down the lake for the journey to Dawson. The NWMP required each boat to bear a number and listed the people in it so checks could be made along the route. If a boat did not show up in a reasonable time at one of the check points, a search was started. Bennett must have looked like a ghost town after this.
UW HEGG 1898

AMHA

UW HEGG

The sternwheelers *Bailey, Clifford Sifton* and *Gleaner* at Lake Bennett, September 1899. YA BARLEY 1899

Caribou Crossing or Carcross during construction of the White Pass and Yukon Route. YA. BARLEY

$190.00 PER WEEK

MADE WITH THE ILLUSTRATED LECTURE OUTFIT ON ALASKA AND THE

KLONDIKE GOLD FIELDS.

SOME MAY HAVE MADE MORE.

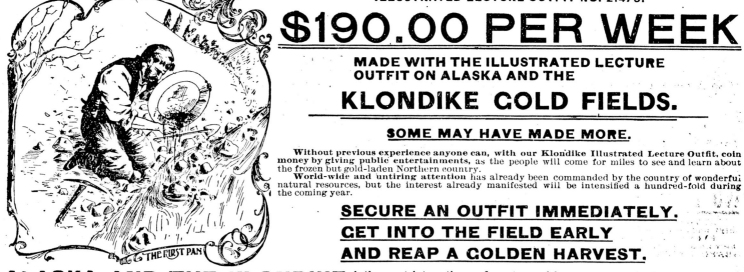

THE FIRST PAN

Without previous experience anyone can, with our Klondike Illustrated Lecture Outfit, coin money by giving public entertainments, as the people will come for miles to see and learn about the frozen but gold-laden Northern country.

World-wide and untiring attention has already been commanded by the country of wonderful natural resources, but the interest already manifested will be intensified a hundred-fold during the coming year.

SECURE AN OUTFIT IMMEDIATELY.
GET INTO THE FIELD EARLY
AND REAP A GOLDEN HARVEST.

ALASKA AND THE KLONDIKE

is the most interesting and most promising country on the face of the globe, and an illustrated lecture on this subject has only to be advertised to draw crowded houses at good prices for admission.

Anyone who can read can deliver the lecture, operate the magic lantern, show the magnificent photographic views which accompany this outfit, and do a successful business from the start.

Everybody is wild with excitement and anxious to learn more about the Gold-Laden Northland. The lecturer will have easy sailing and can make big money almost without effort.

The Klondike Illustrated Lecture outfit gives all the information, illustrates it with Magnificent Photographic Views, magnified to ten feet square or larger, will draw crowded houses every night.

Klondike as a subject has no equal. Never before during our business career have we been in a position to offer such an inducement for money making as is here presented.

THE KLONDIKE ILLUSTRATED
LECTURE OUTFIT CONSISTS OF

50 Magnificent Photographic Views,
1 Polished Wood Case for the Views,
1 Special High-Power Magic Lantern (described on a previous page),
1 Polished Wood Carrying Case for Lantern,
1 Large White Screen (100 square feet),
1 Lecture on Alaska and the Klondike Gold Fields, Bound in Book Form,
1000 Large Illustrated Advertising Posters,
1000 Exhibition Admission Tickets,
1 Printing Outfit for Filling in Dates, etc., all for

$48.75.

PRICE REDUCED FROM $58.75.

SLUICE MINING

Is much the quickest way of separating the gold from the dirt, and when means are at hand to prepare for handling the water, this method is used to very great advantage. **The lecturer explains the different methods of mining and separating the gold from the dirt** and makes plain to each one in the audience those things which before have been, to them, shrouded in mystery, and feel that they are much wiser as a result of their evening's entertainment. While the miners are digging and washing gold in Alaska, the exhibitor can be gathering in a liberal share of the precious metal at the entrance to the churches, opera houses, public halls and school houses, with no risk and no danger.

CHILLCOOT PASS

Represents one of the worst places on the overland route from Dyea. This picture was taken in the summer time, when there was no snow on the Pass, and will give an idea of hardships connected with the **transportation of 1,000 pounds of supplies,** which is the amount required for each man for one year. The pen drawing shown here will give but a faint idea of the detail and the life-like appearance of the photographic picture, as it appears magnified to almost life size on the ten-foot screen.

The enjoyment and appreciation of the audience as these pictures are thrown on the screen, while at the same time each one is being described by the lecturer, can be but feebly imagined.

THE 50 PHOTOGRAPHIC VIEWS

have been taken direct from nature, and when they are projected on the immense screen, which is over ten feet square, they will show to the audience the actual appearance of the country, so natural and so life-like that they will almost feel as though they had been there. The views represent the principal cities and towns of interest, such as Seattle, Juneau, Sitka, Ft. Cudahy, St. Michaels and Dawson City; the stopping places and camps along the route to the gold fields; views of the gold mines, placer and sluice mining, and other very interesting scenes. The views together with the lecture which accompanies the outfit, will create almost unbounded enthusiasm and appreciation.

FOR $5.00

CASH WITH ORDER WE WILL, IF DESIRED, SHIP THE ABOVE OUTFIT C. O. D., SUBJECT TO A THOROUGH EXAMINATION BEFORE PAYING THE BALANCE OF $43.75 AND EXPRESS OR FREIGHT CHARGES.

No. 21475. Complete Outfit, including High Power Magic Lantern, 50 Photographic Views, Screen, Advertising Posters, as described above and on previous pages; everything ready to start work at once.

DESCRIPTION OF MAGIC LANTERN AND OTHER PARTS OF THE OUTFIT SEE PREVIOUS PAGE.

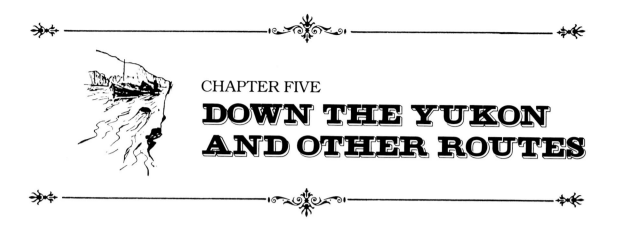

CHAPTER FIVE

DOWN THE YUKON AND OTHER ROUTES

There were many possible routes to the gold fields. The two most popular were the Chilkoot and White Pass trails, but others were used to some degree during the gold rush.

Once the stampeder left Lake Bennett in his boat, he faced a 550-mile water trip before he reached the gold fields. This trip could last several weeks depending on many factors. Several obstacles were in his way before he could get to clear water and a leisurely trip to Dawson.

From Lake Bennett the boat traveled through Marsh Lake and past Tagish Post. This was the largest North West Mounted Police post on the Yukon River and close to 30,000 stampeders checked in here during the summer of 1898.

Miles Canyon was the first major obstacle along the river after the stampeder left Bennett. It was the end of the trip for many who, in their hurry to get down river, tried to ride the water through the narrow canyon. The walls rose more than one hundred feet above the water, which rushed through a narrow opening and created a dangerous whirlpool. If the boat made it through the canyon it had to contend with the Squaw and Whitehorse rapids just below. The rocks, tree roots and sand bars tore the bottom out of many boats and a few people drowned. The Mounted Police finally had to step in and require that women and children walk the five miles around the dangerous water to a point below the rapids. Men experienced in the river were hired to take the boats through for a fee. A tramway, built of wooden rails, was soon constructed, and for $25

When word of the gold rush started to spread, the NWMP established its first post at Tagish on Marsh Lake in 1897 to check incoming prospectors and to assess tariffs. It became the largest police post on the Yukon River, and 200 men checked close to 30,000 people through in that hectic summer of 1898. By 1900 the post was of little use and was abandoned. YA GILLIS 1898

A view of the Tagish Post waterfront in 1898. Thousands of stampeders checked in here before continuing their trip down the Yukon River to Dawson. UW HEGG 1898

The same view today shows no evidence of the frenzied activity on these beaches in the summer of 1898.

RECEIVING MAIL AT TAGISH POST - 1898

With so many people descending on the Yukon in 1897-98, the mail service was totally inadequate. Sometimes men had to wait six months or longer for their mail, and they spent hours reading and rereading letters from friends and family. Sorting of this pile must have taken days, and it is a wonder that the men could wait so patiently.
UW HEGG 1898

Remains of a cabin at Tagish Post, possibly from the gold rush era.

a boat and outfit could be hauled around the canyon and rapids.

Now the river lay open for the final trip to Dawson.

The town of Whitehorse was just beyond the last rapids. It was just beginning to achieve importance as a river boat terminus and later on as the northern terminus of the White Pass and Yukon Railway connecting the town with tidewater at Skagway.

From Whitehorse, the boater floated down through Lake Laberge, past Hootalinqua, Big Salmon and the present site of Carmacks. The next two sets of rapids, Five Finger and Rink, he hardly noticed after what he had already been through. From then on it was an easy trip down river past old Fort Selkirk and Stewart and finally to Dawson, where the Klondike and Yukon Rivers meet.

In that spring and summer of 1898, while thousands of boats were floating down the river from Bennett, others who had been frozen in all winter joined the armada in the race for the gold fields.

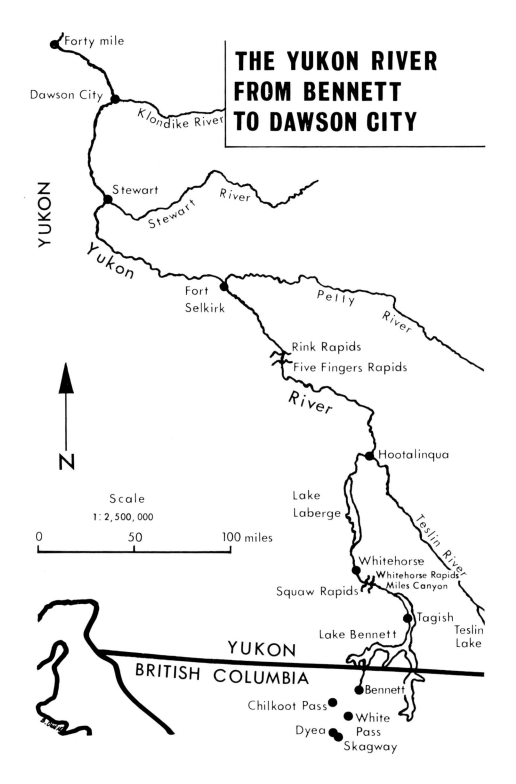

THE YUKON RIVER
FROM BENNETT
TO DAWSON CITY

Forty mile

Dawson City

Klondike River

YUKON

Stewart

Stewart River

Yukon

Fort Selkirk

Pelly River

Rink Rapids

Five Fingers Rapids

River

Hootalinqua

Lake Laberge

Teslin River

N

Scale
1 : 2,500,000
0   50   100 miles

Whitehorse
Whitehorse Rapids
Miles Canyon

Squaw Rapids

Tagish

Lake Bennett

Teslin Lake

YUKON
BRITISH COLUMBIA

Bennett

Chilkoot Pass

White Pass

Dyea

Skagway

Map of the Yukon River from Lake Bennett to Dawson.

Many stampeders braved the rigors of the Chilkoot and White passes only to meet their end at Miles Canyon. Running the white water was a task only the experienced should have tried. The walls of the canyon were up to 100 feet high and a boat had to ride the midriver crest to survive. Jack London piloted several boats through the canyon. YA 1898

The *Clifford Sifton* steaming through turbulent Miles Canyon, July 1900. YA MACBRIDE MUSEUM COLLECTION

Miles Canyon. UW, W & S

Miles Canyon, just below
the city of Whitehorse,
does not look so treach-
erous today. The White-
horse Dam built down-
stream has raised the
level of the river and
calmed it. A footbridge
was built over the can-
yon in the 1920s. The
tour boat *Schwatka* is
shown navigating the
waters.

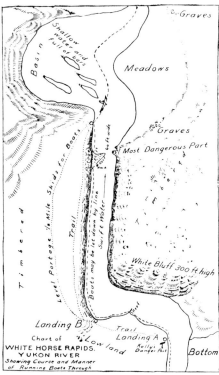

A tramway car with a load on the Canyon and Whitehorse Rapids Tramway. These cars ran on wooden rails around Miles Canyon and Whitehorse Rapids from 1898 to 1900. When the railroad reached Whitehorse in 1900 the river trip was no longer necessary. UW HEGG 1898

The first major river obstacle below Lake Bennett on the Yukon River was Miles Canyon and Whitehorse Rapids. Canyon City was established with the building of the Canyon and Whitehorse Rapids Tramway to haul freight around these dangerous waters. If the stampeder could afford five cents a pound he could save himself considerable risk and work. The tramway was crude but effective. UW CURTIS 1899

An original tramway car now on display at the MacBride Museum in Whitehorse, Yukon.

BY RAIL TO KLONDIKE: POLICE POST AT WHITE HORSE, AND TRAMWAY AROUND MILES CAÑON AND WI

The Illustration, taken in the summer of 1898, shows the landing-place of the Yukon steam-boats, wi.h the steamer " Flora " starting

OPPOSITE TOP: Sternwheelers *Gleaner, Australian* and *Nora* at a dock at the head of Miles Canyon. At this point supplies were loaded onto flat cars of the Whitehorse Tramline and taken around the canyon and Whitehorse Rapids, 1899.
YA HEGG 1899

Two miles below Miles Canyon came the White-horse Rapids. For the inexperienced boatman these rapids were dangerous and caused many to portage or use the tramway. Experienced pilots earned $25 taking a boat through.

YA CURTIS

Drying out after a wreck at Whitehorse Rapids. This incident was typical of the inexperienced stampeders in their rush to get to the gold fields. These men were lucky and probably made it to Dawson.

YA HEGG 1898

CITY OF WHITE HORSE Y.T.

ADAMS & LARKIN PH
DAWSON Y.T.

Whitehorse on the Yukon River in 1900 was a bustling riverport and railroad terminus for the Klondike gold fields 500 miles downriver. In 1898 the town was a cluster of tents and log cabins on the east bank of the Yukon River. When the railroad was completed in July 1900, the town expanded to the west bank.
YA ADAMS & LARKIN 1900

Three views of Whitehorse. The top right is a very early view with few buildings in town. The left photo was taken about 1900 and above in 1930. YA, AHL, UAA

The waterfront of Whitehorse today has lost its riverboats but has become the largest and most important city of the Yukon, with a population of more than 17,000. It is the capital of the territory.

Till I came to the marge of Lake Leberge,
* and a derelict there lay;*
It was jammed in the ice, but I saw in a
* trice it was called the "Alice May"*
And I looked at it, and I thought a bit,
* and I looked at my frozen chum;*
Then "here," said I, with a sudden cry,
* "is my cre-ma-tor-eum."*

Lake Laberge has been immortalized in part of Robert Service's poem "The Cremation of Sam Magee."

Thirty miles below Lake Laberge was Hootalinqua, another stop on the route down the Yukon. A NWMP post was established here in 1898. The telegraph line from Whitehorse to Dawson passed through here. UW HEGG 1898

Five Finger Rapids was the last obstacle on the Yukon before Dawson. After the other rapids, however, Five Finger presented no real problem. The rapids looked like five protruding fingers and most boats made it through with ease. YA

The rapids have not changed since 1898.

The sternwheeler *Whitehorse* passing through Five Finger Rapids, 1904. YA

Fort Selkirk, at the junction of the Yukon and Pelly rivers, had been a post of some type since 1848 when Robert Campbell set up a fort for the Hudson's Bay Company. Arthur Harper established a trading post here in 1889 and during the gold rush the post flourished, with stampeders and cattle stopping here from the Dalton Trail and river routes on their way down to Dawson. The post was practically abandoned in 1951 and today is a historical monument.
UW HEGG

The last stop on the Yukon River before reaching Dawson was at the junction of the Stewart and Yukon rivers. A NWMP post was established here to check the stampeders. Here the gold fields were almost within sight after many months of hardships.
UW HEGG 1898

Meanwhile other routes were put to use as soon as news of the strike reached the outside. The safest and easiest was the all-water route from the West Coast, through the Aleutian Islands to St. Michael, Alaska, on Norton Sound. River boats were then taken up the Yukon River to Dawson. The route was restricted to the summer months when the river was ice-free. It was called the "rich man's" route but the uncertain availability of boats and the distance of more than 4,700 miles made this trip months long.

The Dalton Trail was a series of land routes from the head of Pyramid Harbor, near present-day Haines, Alaska, over the Chilkat Pass to a point on the Yukon River near Five Finger Rapids. It was built by Jack Dalton, who had come north in the 1880s. Dalton charged a toll to use his route and was man enough to enforce collection of the fees. More than 2,000 cattle were driven over the trail in 1898 to help relieve the food shortage in Dawson.

The Klondike Relief Expedition also used the Dalton Trail in 1898. This was a hastily organized effort to relieve the famine in Dawson in the

A cattle drive in 1898 on the Dalton Trail, which was pioneered by Jack Dalton and actually was a series of three trails that led to the interior of the Yukon. The cattle are about to cross the Dezadeash River near the village of Champagne, Yukon. YA BANKS 1898

View of Champagne, Yukon, on the Alaska Highway, 80 miles west of Whitehorse. It has the largest Indian burial ground in the Yukon. One of the Dalton trails went through the village in 1898.

View of St. Michael, Alaska, in the 1890s. This port town near the mouth of the Yukon River was the starting point for the long riverboat journey up the river to Dawson. AHL

View of the North West Mounted Police post at Dalton Post, Yukon, in August 1899. The post was established by Jack Dalton in 1898 and was the main trading post on the Dalton Trail. YA 1899

Remains of Dalton Post, two miles west of the Haines Highway just above the British Columbia border. These buildings were part of the trading post. The NWMP station was built across the river.

winter of 1897-98. A herd of 539 reindeer, brought from Norway, started on the long walk to Dawson in May. Not many made it. By the time remnants of the herd staggered into Dawson in January 1899, the famine was long over and the relief expedition itself needed relief.

Other overland all-year routes were publicized by their backers. Several routes traversed the wilds of the Alaska interior. One went through Valdez and the Cooper River Valley to Fort Yukon and then down the Yukon River to Dawson. One went over the Malaspina Glacier to the Yukon interior. Both of these routes were nearly impossible and many men died using them. From Wrangell, another route went from Alaska, up the Stikine River to Telegraph Creek, British Columbia, then overland toward the lakes and rivers draining northward to the Yukon.

The Canadians, meanwhile, were pushing their own routes to promote a spirit of patriotism and to further their own business interests.

The Ashcroft route started in British Columbia and cut through more than 1,000 miles of the wilds of the Province to Telsin Lake. The whole trail turned into a sea of mud and few stampeders made it to Dawson by this route.

The businessmen of the small town of Edmonton, Alberta, pushed their route and made it sound like a picnic. Actually, several trails started there and traversed some of the most desolate country on the continent. Although the routes were advertised as being well marked, they were in reality nothing at all and most of the people had to blaze their own trails. One route led down the Athabasca River to Great Slave Lake, then down the Mackenzie River, above the Arctic Circle, to Fort McPherson and then down to Dawson. This was a distance of more than 2,500 miles. Several other routes went overland part way to the Liard and Peel rivers and then down the Yukon River.

Few of the people starting out on these so-called routes ever made it to Dawson, and the ones who did arrived in the spring of 1899 as the rush was coming to an end. Tales of the journeys through this country read like horror stories and even the lure of gold was not enough to keep the people going.

With the completion of the railroad over White Pass, most of the other routes were abandoned. But by that time the main gold rush was over and new routes were being charted to the new gold discovery at Nome, Alaska.

The Chilkoot and White Pass trails and the all-water route were also used when the stampeder left the gold fields for the outside with his fortune or with nothing.

Outfitting for the Klondike at the Hudson's Bay Company Store in Edmonton, Alberta, in 1898.
PROVINCIAL ARCHIVES OF ALBERTA

Stampeders building boats on the Athabasca River in northern Alberta for the long voyage to
Dawson. PROVINCIAL ARCHIVES OF ALBERTA

After the rush was over and the railroad was completed to Whitehorse in 1900, stage routes were set up between Whitehorse and Dawson. Wagons were used in the summer and sleds in the winter, and the trip was reduced to only a few days. With the building of the Alaska Highway in 1942. Yukon was open to vehicular traffic from the outside. YA

Remains of Montague House, 22 miles south of Carmacks on the Klondike Highway. This was a rest stop on the stage route from Whitehorse to Dawson in the early 1900s. One of the Dalton trails ended at this point.

One of the White Pass and Yukon Stage Line wagons now on display at Carcross, Yukon.

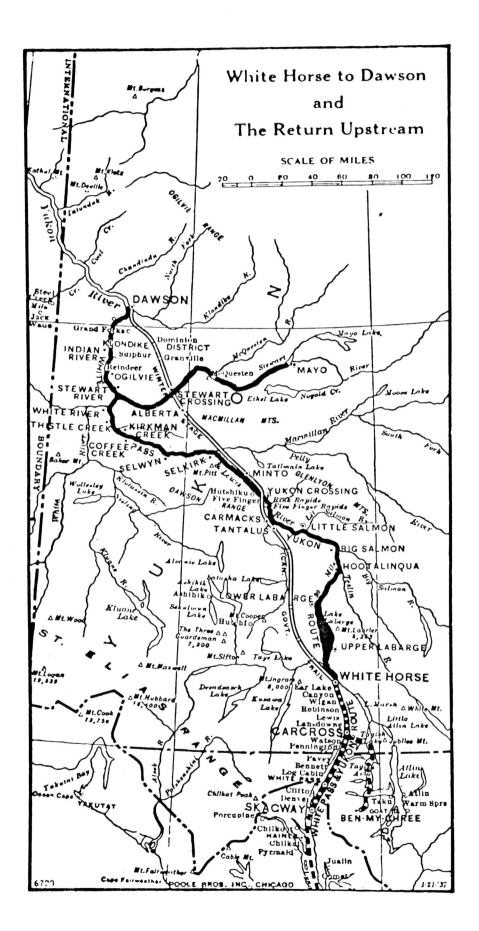

White Horse to Dawson

and

The Return Upstream

SCALE OF MILES

This map shows the river route from Lake Bennett to Dawson City, the railway route of the White Pass & Yukon Route from Bennett to Whitehorse and the winter stage trail from Whitehorse to Dawson City. The W.P. & Y.R. train closed in 1982. The last regularly scheduled voyage was made by the sternwheeler *Klondike* in August 1955. The *Klondike* is restored and rests on the bank of the Yukon River in Whitehorse. It is open to the public daily. The Yukon Stage Line was owned by the W.P. & Y.R. and operated the winter transportation system between Whitehorse and Dawson City using horse-drawn sleighs from 1901 through 1921. Horses were used by their successors for one season and thereafter winter transportation was conducted by various contractors using trucks and Caterpillar tractors hauling sleighs and cabooses. After 1937 all mail, passengers and freight were carried by airplane until the construction of the all-weather Klondike Highway in 1955. YA

Brochures were printed each year promoting tourism in Alaska and the Yukon. YA

Panoramic view of the British Yukon Navigation Company's fleet dry-docked for the winter at the Whitehorse shipyards in 1901. At least twelve sternwheelers are shown. UW

The ill-fated *Columbian* was built in Victoria, B.C., in 1898 and used on the upper river run. On Sept. 25, 1906, she was destroyed on the river between Big and Little Salmon when a crew member, shooting at some ducks from the boat, fired into the boat, which was carrying explosives. The resultant explosion and fire killed six crew members. It was the worst accident ever to occur on the river. UW W&S

The *White Horse* docked at Dawson in the early 1900s. UW NOWELL

Disembarking passengers and freight at Dawson. UW HEGG

View of the *Canadian, Columbian* and *Victorian* at the Dawson dock, 1899. YA WOODSIDE 1899

In the early days the steamboats were fueled by wood, and stops had to be made frequently to re-supply the hungry boilers. A steamer could burn 120 cords of four-foot wood on a trip from St. Michael upriver to Dawson.
AMHA & YA

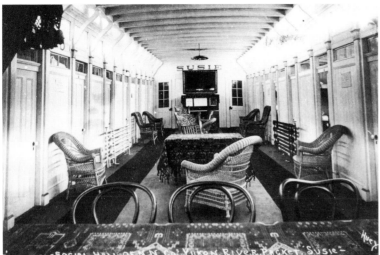

The "social hall" or sitting room of the *Suzie.*
UAA W.F. ERSKINE COLLECTION

The dining salon of the steamer *Alaska.*
AHL R.N. DeARMOND COLLECTION

Passengers on the *Susie.*
UAA

Officers and crew of the *Bailey* pose for a group picture on the top deck of the sternwheeler in August 1899. YA BARLEY

Eagle, Alaska, in the 1890s. The town was established as a military, judicial, and communications and transportation center and was important after the gold rush because of the military post established in 1899, Fort Egbert, which maintained law and order on the Alaskan frontier. YA

At least six sternwheelers are shown wintering at the "Dawson Slough" across from Dawson in 1905-06. YA

Remains of the first *Casca* at Lower Laberge. It was beached here after being used as a barge for many years.
GOVERNMENT OF THE YUKON

The *Casca* No. 3 and the *White Horse* burning at Whitehorse on June 21, 1974. The fire was the work of an arsonist and resulted in a great historical loss to the citizens of the Yukon.
WHITEHORSE STAR

The *Tutshi* and *Gleaner* docked at Carcross in the 1920s.
YA DENNETT COLLECTION

At 1,042 tons, the *Tutshi* was one of the larger boats in the Yukon. She was built at Carcross in 1918, and her original run was between Carcross and Grahame Inlet on Tagish Lake. She was later converted to an oil burner and carried tourists to Ben-My-Chree at the southern tip of Taku Arm. The boat was restored by Parks Canada, but burned to the ground in 1990.

A riverboat graveyard a few miles downriver from Dawson. None of the original boats from the gold rush era have survived, but several newer ones have been preserved. More than 250 steamboats plied the Yukon River from the late 1890s to the early 1950s. They were the lifeblood of the river and hauled freight and passengers to the rich gold fields. By the early '50s the motor vehicle and airplane had replaced the slower river boats. These photos were taken in the 1980s and now very little is left of the boats.

One of the newer boats on the river, the *Keno*, was built in 1922 as a side stream freight hauler. In 1937 it was made ten feet longer to accommodate more freight. It mainly worked the shallow Stewart River, hauling silver-lead-zinc concentrates from Mayo to Stewart City, a distance of 180 miles. There, larger boats picked up the freight for the final trip upriver to Whitehorse. In 1951 it was retired from the river and laid up in dry dock at Whitehorse. Then in 1960 it was donated by the B.Y.N. Co. to the Canadian government and made the last downstream run of any boat to its permanent dry land home at Dawson. YA DENNETT COLLECTION

The sternwheeler *Keno*, docked at Dawson, is under restoration by Parks Canada.

The *Klondike* No. 2 on display at Whitehorse. This was the second boat named *Klondike* and was built in 1937 from part of the wreckage of the first boat. The *Klondike* No. 2 was used to haul freight and passengers on the Yukon between White-horse and Dawson. Due to competition from highways the boat was con-verted into a tourist boat in 1954 and operated for two seasons. In 1966 it was placed on display at Whitehorse and com-pletely restored to its 1937 look by Parks Canada.

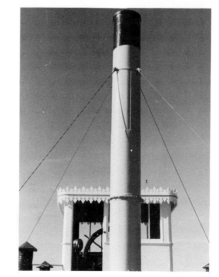

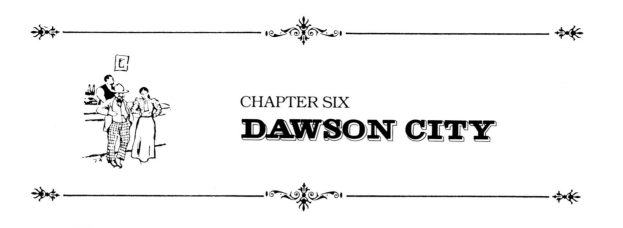

CHAPTER SIX

DAWSON CITY

Little did Dr. George Dawson, a Canadian government geologist, realize that the city Joseph Ladue named after him would become in less than two years the greatest boom town in North America. It would be the largest city north of Vancouver and west of Winnipeg, would be known as the "Paris of the North," and would be the richest city in Canada. What was a swampy moose pasture at the confluence of the Klondike and Yukon rivers in 1896 would be all these things by the summer of 1898. The more common name for Dawson City would be simply Dawson.

Joseph Ladue, an oldtimer in the Yukon, had the foresight to see that the thousands of stampeders expected to come to the area would need a town in which to spend their new wealth. The moose pasture appeared to be the perfect spot and he staked a townsite claim there for himself. He started back to Fortymile to record his claim but came across a man who wanted to buy some lumber to build a house, and Ladue

quickly suspected that increased demand was imminent. He had previously set up a sawmill south of the Dawson site, and, sending his claim notice ahead with a friend, he turned around and traveled to the mill. He packed it up, set it up in Dawson and went into the lumber business. The townsite paid off for him and soon lots on Main Street were selling for several thousand dollars a front foot.

Boats arrived at Dawson continually during the late summer and fall of 1896, and the town began to grow. Ladue's sawmill, warehouse and a cabin which doubled as a saloon were busy all the time. He was not to lose his town as Captain Moore had lost Skagway.

By the spring of 1897, more than 1,500 people lived in Dawson and as soon as the ice broke in the river in May, more poured in. The greatest influx of stampeders was still a year away but already people in Dawson were getting rich. In six months prices tripled or quadrupled. The saloons, dance halls and gambling halls were

Even a year after gold was discovered, Dawson was still a collection of tents and a few log and frame buildings. Things would be different by the summer of 1898. UW 1897

Dawson was still a tent city in early 1898. Tents were set up for every conceivable business, from saloons to dentists' offices. The floors were made out of the boards from the stampeders' boats, and some of the tents were made of the sails. Everyone was on the move, looking for the gold at the end of the rainbow. YA 1898

The Dawson waterfront in the summer of 1898 was a busy place with stampeders coming in from Lake Bennett and St. Michael, river boats bringing in supplies for the creeks and gold being shipped to the outside.
YA 1898

The only craft using the river today are several tourist boats, some fishing boats and an occasional native canoe. River travel ceased in the 1950s with the advent of improved road and air transportation.

Waiting to record their mining claims after standing in line three days, 1897. AMHA

By October 1897 more substantial buildings were being erected in town. AMHA

Waiting for the first mail of the season, March 3, 1898. It left Seattle on November 2, 1897. AMHA

Mining exchange, 1897. AMHA

The upper end of Dawson in 1897 when it was still mainly a tent town. AMHA

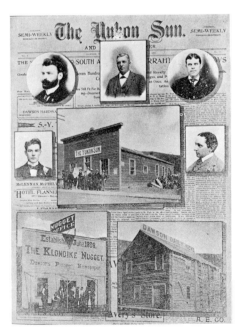

Between 1896 and 1899, Dawson had grown from a mud flat to the largest Canadian city north of Vancouver and west of Winnipeg, with a population of more than 30,000. For one year—from June 1898, to July 1899 —it was one of the grandest cities in North America, where one could do or buy most anything that one had money for.

YA 1900
BETTMANN ARCHIVE/NEW YORK

Dawson today is a town with a
population of over 1,000 people
engaged in commerce, tourism
and placer gold mining.
YUKON TERRITORY TOURISM AND
INFORMATION BRANCH—WHITEHORSE

making fortunes even though most were still doing business in tents.

As winter approached and the Yukon River froze, the threat of starvation loomed. Food was running low and the town came to a standstill. The authorities cautioned everyone against going north until supplies could get in that spring. The United States Congress organized a Klondike Relief Expedition in hope of helping the situation. All through the winter people were on meager rations and it was not until the spring of 1898 that enough supplies could get through. No one starved that winter, but only because many men had left the town in the fall.

When the first boats arrived at Dawson from the winter encampment at Lake Bennett the people in town beseiged the new arrivals for news from outside. They had had no contact with the outside world for more than six months and a newspaper, no matter how old, was worth a lot. In April 1898, 1,600 newspapers, seven months old, were brought to town and sold for one dollar each. The most important news was that thou

A "Mountie" on his mount in Dawson.
YA FAULKNER COLLECTION

Sam Steele was the commander of the North West Mounted Police in the North in 1898 and was called the "Lion of the Yukon" for his firm but honest rule of the gold rush. He enforced the order—which saved many lives—that every person entering the Yukon have a year's worth of supplies. He went on to become a general in World War I and a British knight. UW

sands of stampeders were heading downriver for Dawson at that very moment.

By the summer of 1898, Dawson had a population of more than 30,000 and people were constantly on the move. Excitement was in the air and in the long days of the northern summer the town was open 24 hours a day. Banks, newspapers, theaters, churches, businesses and even a telephone line were established, and new wooden buildings, replacing the tents, were going up everywhere. Prices fluctuated daily with supply and demand. Many people made fortunes in scarce necessities like condensed milk, rubber boots, brooms and nails. The streets of Dawson were paved with gold for these merchants and they did not have to set foot on a mining claim to strike it rich.

An article in the *Klondike Nugget* on July 8, 1898, provides an example of Dawson prices:

THIRTY DOLLARS A GALLON
The first milk cow ever in Dawson arrived on Wednesday. She was not very well pleased with her surroundings and did not give much milk, but that first milking brought in just $30 in Klondike dust. She will be treated to the best that Dawson affords—flour and packing-case hay—and is expected to do better as the days grow shorter. One hundred dollars a milking is not too much to expect of her, as she comes of good family and will not do anything to make her ancestors turn over in their graves—or, more properly speaking, in the stomachs of

their patrons. H. I. Miller is the man who brought her in along with 19 male companions. The gentleman is more favorably known as "Cow Miller, and as Cow Miller let him be known from this on."

Some prices in the summer of 1898 were: oranges and lemons from 50 cents to $1.30 each; champagne $20 to $40 a pint; mineral water $3 a bottle; shave $1; haircut $1.50; bath $2.50 and nails $1 a pound. Wages during that summer were $1 to $1.50 per hour for ordinary miners $15 per day for bartenders, $17.50 per day for bookkeepers, $20 per day for faro dealers, $100 per week plus board for cooks, $50 per week plus board for waiters and $15 to $40 per day for barbers. Later that summer, with an increase in the number of men looking for work, the wages of ordinary miners dropped to 60 cents per hour.

Although Dawson was in Canada, its population was 90 percent American, with the other 10 percent divided among Canadians and other nationalities. The North West Mounted Police (now called the Royal Canadian Mounted Police or "Mounties") controlled the town and because of this, it escaped the lawlessness of Skagway. With thousands of people from all over the world and every type of character converging on the town during 1898, it is a real tribute to the police that they maintained order.

Fort Herchmer was built by the police in 1897 as headquarters in Dawson and by 1900, 300 men were on duty in town and in the mining areas.

The boom continued to a lesser degree through the summer of 1899, but by that time gold had been discovered in Nome, Alaska, and Atlin, British Columbia, and the big mining companies were moving into the creeks and putting the individual claim operator out of business. By 1900, Dawson had become a stable mining community. The great gold rush was over and there would never be another like it.

Barracks and officers' cabins of the North West Mounted Police in Dawson. AMHA

The North West Mounted Police were the real heroes of the gold rush. While thousands of men streamed toward the gold fields, these men enforced the law, collected customs, and cared for the sick and destitute, while men around them were becoming millionaires. These men made the Yukon a safe place to live and work compared to the American camps. The first detachment of police arrived in the Yukon at Fortymile in 1894. It was reinforced after the rush started, until by 1900 the force numbered over 300 in the territory.
AHL GOETZMAN

The Yukon Field Force drilling at Fort Herchmer in Dawson in 1900. The fort was built in 1897 by the North West Mounted Police for its headquarters. The Yukon Field Force was sent to Dawson to help the police maintain order in the predominantly American population. UW L & D 1900

Stampeders selling their supplies on the waterfront of Dawson. Perhaps they needed money to survive in Dawson or perhaps they were selling out to return south. Either way they were unlikely to strike it rich. Only about 4,000 prospectors who made it to Dawson grew wealthy, and no more than a hundred held onto their money in the years after the rush. UW CURTIS 1898

Panorama view of Dawson looking east from across the Yukon River. Prominent buildings are from left to right; along Front St.—Fire Department No. 2; Government House; N.W.M.P. Barracks and Grounds; Territorial Court Buildings. 2nd Avenue left to right: St. Andrews Presbyterian Church and Parsonage and the Administration Building and Grounds, 1901. YA

Klondike City, across the Klondike River from Dawson, was the site of an old Indian salmon camp and was known as "Lousetown." In the early 1900s it was the site of a large sawmill.
UW CURTIS 1902

OPPOSITE PAGE:
Street scenes in early Dawson. The fire department kept in constant training because of the everpresent threat of fire. Dawson was a typical boom town—frame buildings and tents, boardwalks and muddy streets. One could almost sink out of sight in the streets after a heavy rain.
UW L & D 1898

The "ladies of the night" caused problems and they were moved to their own district, called "Oshiwora," 'White Chapel" or "Lousetown," at Klondike City, across the Klondike River from Dawson. There was only a narrow footbridge to carry customers across the river. Some drunks had trouble negotiating it. UW L&D

First Canadian mail leaves Dawson, March 5, 1898, 24 dogs, 6 men, 6000 lbs. letters. AMHA

Paying with Gold Dust.   Fall 1899.

Gold was worth $16 an ounce if clean, but if laced with black sand or brass filings brought far less. Gold dust from a miner's poke was weighed on gold scales and then exchanged for merchandise or services. As men became richer, price became immaterial; there was more gold than could be spent in a lifetime, or so people thought.
UW L & D 1899

The streets of Dawson were a sea of mud after a rainstorm. UW

CAPT. ... WFORD ENTERTAINING THE KLONDYKERS

The well-known American cowboy and Indian fighter, Captain Jack Crawford, giving a speech at the July 4, 1899, celebration. With up to 90 percent of the stampeders U.S. citizens, Dawson was an American town in character. Only the Mounties kept it from becoming another center of lawlessness like Skagway.
UW HEGG 1899

One and one-half tons of gold await shipment in 1901 at the Alaska Commercial Company office in Dawson. At today's price this would be worth millions of dollars.
UW HEGG 1901

Gamblers pose at a table in Dawson. Gambling was the favorite pastime of the miners. Every form of gambling was in evidence and men would bet on anything. Stakes at the poker tables ran as high as $50,000 and many a casino changed hands on the flip of a card. AHL GOETZMAN

A crowd waits for the mail in the summer of 1898. This log building was Dawson's fourth post office. UW HEGG 1898

Dawson, less than 200 miles south of the Arctic Circle, had harsh winters. Temperatures as low as 80°F below zero were recorded near Dawson during the gold rush. The oldtimers measured the cold by liquids that froze at different temperatures. Kerosene froze at -35° to -55°F, according to grade; pain killer at -72°F; St. Jacobs oil at -75°F and Hudsons Bay Rum at -80°F. When the dog-freighter's mercury froze at -40°F he didn't travel. UW CANTWELL

Indians selling
moosemeat in Dawson.
Food was in short supply,
especially in the winter of
1897-98. AMHA

At the height of the rush
you could buy almost
anything in Dawson from
the finest Paris fashions
to the best champagne to
freshly killed game. Any-
thing was for sale for
enough gold. If you did
not strike it rich on the
creeks but had good luck
and fortitude, you might
make a fortune as a mer-
chant, showman or bar
owner. Some of the rich-
est men went south with
money made on the
streets of Dawson rather
than on the creeks. The
streets were paved with
gold if you knew how to
mine them.

AHL GOETZMAN 1901

Looking up Front Street
from the Northern Com-
mercial Company store.
This building has been
reconstructed in its
original location for use
as a visitors center by
Parks Canada and the
Klondike Visitors'
Association.

BETTMANN ARCHIVE/NEW YORK

PRESENT-DAY DAWSON SCENES

More old buildings in Dawson.

St. Paul's Church dates from 1902. It has been in constant use since then.

Some buildings, such as this hardware store, seem to be standing in defiance of nature. This much-photographed structure has deteriorated since this photo was taken.

The Yukon Hotel has been restored by Parks Canada.

Some of the old abandoned houses in town.

St. Andrews Church was built in 1901. It is in a bad state of repair.

Third Avenue looking north with the giant earth slide on the hillside.

Jack London's cabin. The "Ghost of Jack London" returns each summer to his cabin in Dawson. He is famous for his northern adventure books.

Harrington's Store on Third Avenue and Princess Street is now used by Parks Canada to portray the story of the gold rush.

The Dawson City Museum is located in the 1901 territorial government building. It was restored by the government in 1986 and court is still held in the upstairs court chambers.

Engines from the Klondike Mines Railway on display in Dawson at the Territorial Museum. The railway was built from Dawson to the gold fields in 1906 to provide an easier way to ship in supplies and ship out gold. It was discontinued in 1914. A shed now covers these historic engines.

Because of poor construction and several fires there are few buildings left from the gold rush days. Most of the older buildings were built in the early 1900s after the city had established itself as more than just a temporary town. Many new replica buildings have been built in the last few years, including this reconstruction of the Red Feather Saloon.

The Arctic Brotherhood Hall was built about 1900 and was used for many social and fraternal functions. YA

With the passing of the oldtimers, the Arctic Brotherhood became Diamond Tooth Gertie's Gambling Hall. The only legal gambling establishment in Canada, it operates during the summer tourist season.

Can Can girls still dance on the stage of Diamond Tooth Gertie's.

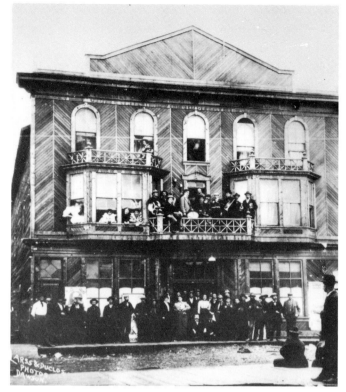

The Palace Grand Theater, built by Arizona Charlie Meadows, a famous cowboy and trick shooter, was the grandest entertainment palace in the Yukon when it opened in July 1899. Meadows built the building with material taken from several beached sternwheelers. It offered every type of entertainment from wild west shows to opera. After 1900 the theater fell into disrepair, but it was saved from destruction by the Klondike Visitors' Association.
UW L&D

The theater was reconstructed in the 1960s and now offers the nightly Gaslight Follies in the summer tourist season. One gets the feeling that Arizona Charlie Meadows is still roaming the interior watching after the shows.

Life in Dawson wasn't dull. This photo shows the interior of the Palace Grand Theater in 1898 during the St. Andrew's Ball. Dawson became a very social city, with clubs for practically any form of entertainment, education or sports. YA & D 1898

A Carnegie Library was built in 1903 and was to be the envy of many other towns for years.
YA CHISHOLM

In later years the library became a Masonic Hall and today has been restored and is still in use as a fraternal hall.

The first government building to be built in Dawson was the post office, which opened in November 1900. It also housed other government offices and finally closed in 1924. Before 1900 the post office was shifted from a tent to a succession of buildings. Service was poor because the federal government did not think the rush would last long enough to pay for complete postal services or a permanent building. Efficiency increased with construction of this building. The post office today is an exact reconstruction of the original building and still offers some postal services. UW HEGG

The new courthouse was built in 1901, when Dawson was the government center for the entire territory. The courthouse has been reconstructed and is used for territorial government offices. YA ADAMS & LARKIN

The commissioner's residence on Front Street was a fancy building when it was completed around 1901. It was one of a number of buildings built after the rush was over to house the Yukon government offices and officials. The building was damaged by fire in 1905 and rebuilt. It was the official residence of the commissioner from 1901 to 1916. It has been restored by Parks Canada. YA 1901

The first Canadian Bank of Commerce was housed in this log building. In 1899 the present building was built on the banks of the Yukon. Later tin siding was added for the look the building has now. YA & AMHA

The Canadian Bank of Commerce, shown here, and the Bank of North America raced each other to Dawson in 1898. The latter won, but both did a booming business shipping the gold outside. Paper money was exchanged for the gold dust as it was less cumbersome to handle. YA WOODSIDE

The Bank of Commerce building on the water-front has been closed for several years.

The Bank of North America at the corner of Second Avenue and Queen Street won the race to Dawson in the summer of 1898 and did a thriving business for many years. The bank building today has been restored to its original look. UW ELLINGSEN

The old Indian village of Moosehide just west of Dawson in 1900. One legend has it that the Indians moved from the site of Dawson at the time of the big slide whose scars are still visible from town. More probably they moved when the white man started moving into Dawson. This village was quite large at the time of the gold rush, but after 1900 the Indians moved back to Dawson to work and most of the buildings were torn down. YA 1900

Remains of Moosehide. Only a few old houses remain along with the Anglican church, used by Bishop Bompas to convert the Indians to Christianity, and the old schoolhouse.

CHAPTER SEVEN

THE CREEKS

The first news of the gold rush was like a dream come true. A prospector, it was said, had only to scrape up the gold in the pan and he would be rich. Gold was so plentiful that it would last forever. But in truth, the dream had not quite come true. After getting his outfit together, fighting for a place on one of the north bound ships, struggling over the passes, spending the winter at Lake Bennett, building a boat and then floating 550 miles down the Yukon, the stampeder found when he reached the Klondike that conditions were not as ideal as he had been led to expect.

Most of the good ground had been claimed by the prospectors who were already on the scene in 1896 and early 1897. By the time of the massive influx of people, in the summer of 1898, nothing was left to stake. The new arrivals either worked for wages on the creeks, found jobs in Dawson or sold their outfits and returned home in disgust.

The gold field area comprised 800 square miles from the Klondike River on the north to the Indian River on the south and from the Yukon River on the west to Flat and Dominion creeks on the east. In this area were some of the richest deposits of gold ever found.

The gold was deposited as "placer" or free gold, as opposed to lode gold which is embedded in rock. The gold-bearing rocks of the region date from early in the geologic time scale (more than 400 million years ago) and are mainly of igneous origin. Much later in geologic time these rocks were eroded and the gold, being very heavy, settled in the stream gravels. Later the land was uplifted and the streams caused a rapid erosion that concentrated the gold-bearing gravels on the underlying bedrock. The gold was found in three distinct levels in the area: in the ancient stream beds or white channels, 100 to 300 feet above the present creek beds; on benches above the valley floor; and in the beds of the existing creeks.

Glaciation, so destructive to land in the north, had not occurred in the Klondike area because of its semi-arid nature, so the high gold concentration on bedrock was left intact. The extreme cold also helped prevent rapid erosion of the gold.

The site of the first gold discovery on August 17, 1896, on Bonanza Creek, about 12 miles from Dawson City.

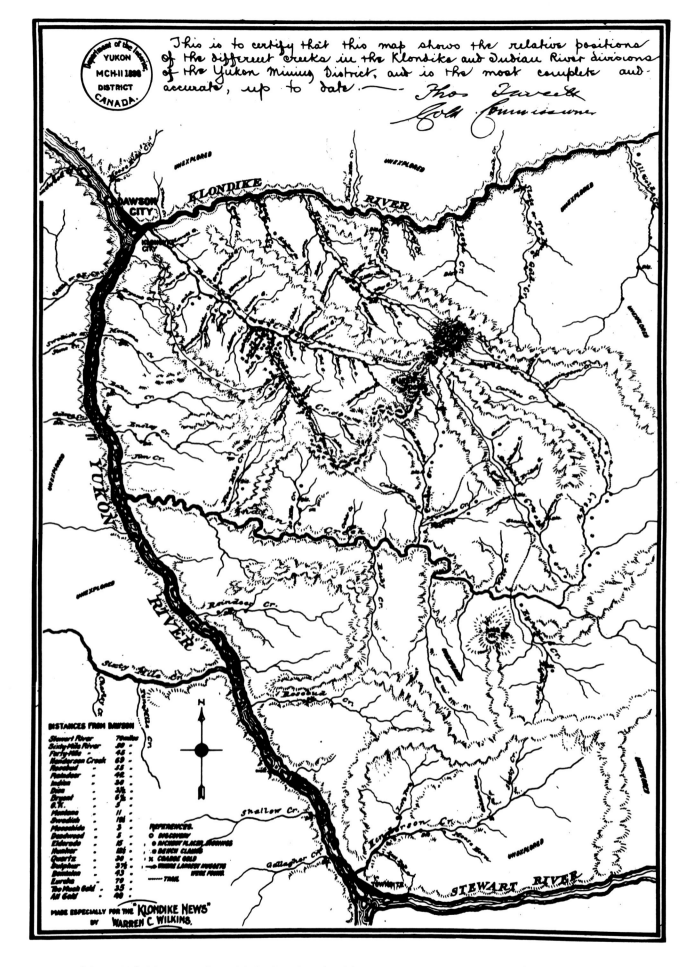

Map of the gold fields originally published in the Klondike News in 1898. The extent of the workings can be seen by the distances from Dawson City.

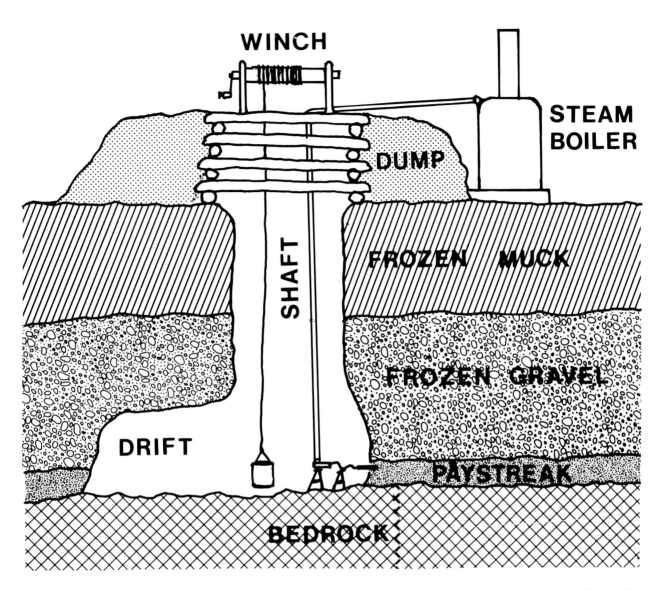

Early mining method. Fire or steam was used to dig a shaft to bedrock through the frozen muck and gravel. The paystreak, if present, was on the bedrock. A drift was dug along the paystreak and the gold bearing gravel was hauled to the surface with the windlass and stockpiled till spring.

In seeking placer gold the individual miner could work a small area with a few tools and small investment. This was known as "poor man's mining."

Canadian mining laws were in effect in the area from the very first discovery. In the United States foreigners could not stake mining claims, but in Canada anyone could stake a claim. This explains why so many American citizens headed north.

One person could stake one claim, or two, if he made an initial discovery in a mining district. The entire Klondike area was considered one mining district. Any number of people could work their claims in common and claims could be bought and sold at will. As stated by Canadian Mining Law:

Creek and river claims shall be 500 feet long, measured in the direction of the general course of the stream and shall extend in width from base to base of the hill or bench on each side. When the hill or benches are less than 100 feet apart, the claim may be 100 feet in depth. The sides of a claim shall be two parallel lines run as nearly as possible at right angles to the stream. The sides shall be marked with legal posts at or about the edge of the water and at the rear boundaries of the claim. One of the legal posts at the stream shall be legibly marked with the name of the miner and the date upon which the claim was staked.

Underground mining was hard, dirty work, but a few were rewarded with great wealth. These men appear to be mining the pay streak just above bedrock. Every inch had to be steam-thawed, mucked by hand, hauled up the shaft by windlass and piled until spring. These were intolerable working conditions—poor light, stale air, low temperatures and cramped working quarters—but the lure of gold made up for the conditions. UW CANTWELL

After a claim was located, the miner had three days to record it with the local gold commissioner if the claim was within ten miles of the recording office. He had one additional day for every additional ten miles of distance. The entry fee was $15 and another fee varying from $15 to $100 was charged for each additional year that the claim was held. In addition the government imposed a 10 percent royalty on gold taken from a claim up to $500 a week, and 20 percent on gold above this amount.

Claims were recorded by numbers above and below the initial discovery on each creek: #1 Above Bonanza, #40 Below Eldorado, and so forth.

The freedom to buy or lease as many claims as he could afford formed the basis of many an enterprising miner's fortune. There are countless stories of claim stakers, thinking their claims worthless, leasing or selling out for practically nothing and then discovering that just a few feet below the surface a fortune in gold was deposited. Many men leased out or let a "lay" on their claims, and without ever working themselves made great amounts of money.

The early claim stakers found the rich deposits by simply panning along the streams. Soon after the first discovery in August 1896, creeks for miles around were staked, and the new arrivals had to prospect farther and farther from Dawson. By the summer of 1898, when the mass exodus north was at its height, most of the rich stream bed deposits had been discovered and staked for

Many means of reducing the burdens of mining were tried. Even dogs were used to haul the ore to the bottom of the shaft. After 1899 it was no longer practical to mine this way and a more efficient method had to be devised to move large quantities of gravel. By then, hydraulic mining and dredging were just coming into use. YA CANTWELL

UW

Great quantities of wood were needed to keep the thawing fires going in the holes. The photo on the right shows a new hole being started, all by hand labor, through frozen ground. AMHA

A windlass lowering a miner into his mine hole.
AMHA

All through the winter the creeks took on an eerie look with the smoking holes on the different claims. This is at the forks of Eldorado and Bonanza creeks. AMHA

a total distance of 85 miles. Creek names like Bonanza, Eldorado, Hunker, Too Much Gold, Gold Bottom, Sulphur, Dominion, Adams, French and others had become world-famous. The Klondike had become synonymous with adventure and great wealth.

Several early miners thought that the richest gold would lie on bedrock at some depth below ground surface. In the fall of 1896, Louis Rhodes, who was laughed at for digging his way to bedrock, struck it rich at the 15-foot depth and from then on everyone started working his claim to bedrock. Where in the past a pan worth ten cents was considered good, miners were now getting pans worth hundreds of dollars. When news like this reached the outside world, thousands started for the Klondike.

The gold at bedrock was covered by a layer of decayed organic matter called muck and a layer of permanently frozen gravel below the muck, so some method had to be found to get to the pay streak. A method devised at Fortymile in 1887 involved burning a shaft down to bedrock by a succession of fires that thawed the ground deeper and deeper. Then a drift or lateral was thawed along the pay streak, and the dirt was hauled to the surface by bucket and windlass and stockpiled until spring, when it could be washed through a sluice box. Every so often the pay streak had to be panned to make certain it still contained gold. This was a slow, hard way to mine and there was no assurance that after spending months digging his way to bedrock, a miner would strike the pay streak.

Men using rockers on Gold Hill. Rockers were a gold separation device used where water was in short supply. UW CURTIS

A windlass in operation on one of the claims on French Hill. The thawed pay dirt was hauled up the shaft by this simple but backbreaking machine and dumped until it could be washed through the sluice boxes in the spring. UW HEGG

The hard work of bringing up the gold-laden gravel went on regardless of the weather. The gold was there for those who wanted to work for it. UW

A fifty dollar pan. Today this would be a fantastic find. YA MIZONY

Miners using rockers on King Solomon's Hill in 1898. YA ADAMS & LARKIN 1898

Clarence Berry, one of
the early claim stakers
and eventually one of the
richest miners in the area,
is shown here on #6
Above, on Eldorado
Creek, shoveling dirt into
a lady's gold pan.
YA GLENBOLD 1897

Clarence Berry's claims
on Eldorado Creek, 1898.
AMHA

Steam thawing eventually replaced the wood burning as it was much more efficient. Steam points were driven into the frozen ground and steam was piped down to them from boilers on the surface. This method of mining was used only in the winter because summer brought the danger of cave-ins from melting ground, and summer also was the only time of year water was available to wash the mounds of gold-laden gravels through sluice boxes.

Until 1900 this method was practical for the individual miner, because it required little capital and little else except willingness to work long hours in harsh conditions. The rich deposits were soon worked out, however, and new methods and increasingly expensive machinery had to be devised to extract the gold.

While thousands of miners were digging their way to bedrock on the main stream beds, a few individuals looked up at the hillsides along the creek valleys and decided to try their luck prospecting there. They were laughed at, and one hill was named after the Indian word for tenderfoot—"Cheechaco Hill." But in 1897, French Hill, Gold Hill, Cheechaco Hill and all the hills up and down Bonanza Creek were found to have gold in ancient stream channels, and a second rush was on. Every square inch of the benches and hillsides was staked. There seemed to be no end to the gold in the Klondike.

With the number of miners increasing daily on the creeks in the Klondike valleys, several towns were built so the miners did not have to go to Dawson for their supplies and entertainment. Some grew to considerable size, with Grand Forks at the confluence of Bonanza and Eldorado creeks becoming the largest. Many people grew wealthy serving the miners with stores, saloons, and gambling halls, and by hauling supplies and gold to and from Dawson.

The stories of the richness of these claims and the luck and frustrations of the individuals who made their way to the Klondike have filled many books. Men became millionaires overnight on the chance purchase of a claim someone thought gold-barren. Some won their claims in the gambling halls of Dawson or were given an interest in a claim for grubstaking a friend. However, the day of the individual who could be rich on the turn of a shovel was over in a very short time.

In 1896 the Klondike creeks produced $300,000 worth of gold; in 1897, $2,500,000; in 1898, $10,000,000; in 1899, $16,000,000 and in 1900, $22,275,000. Gold at that time was worth $16 an ounce.

Sluice boxes on Eldorado Creek. When spring came and water was available, the mine dumps were run through the sluice boxes to separate the gold from the gravels. UW CURTIS

View of extensive workings on Upper Eldorado Creek, showing mine dumps, water systems and miners' tents. Every inch of this creek was staked and fabulous fortunes were made here. UW CURTIS 1898

Living conditions were miserable in the miners' cabins. In the winter the cabin had to be heated all the time; in the summer the mosquitos took over. The quarters were cramped, food was bland and nerves were at the breaking point most of the time. The men in the picture on the left are probably splitting up their gold from a cleanup. The picture on the right shows the men at their dinner table. The haze in the picture is probably from smoke in the cabin and not faulty photography.

The miners' cabins on their claims were crude. The men had time for little but digging for gold. They had to put up with bitter cold in winter, insects in summer and their own temperaments the year 'round. It was no life for weaklings. UW CHILD

Most of the miners had left their families at home and hoped to return soon, as wealthy men. Life was rough and men had to learn to do for themselves. UW HEGG

Interior of the 16 Mile Roadhouse on the Yukon River. Quarters were cramped but at least there was heat and hot food available for the weary traveler. YA

MINING APPARATUS

A close-up view of a gold rocker. These devices were used where water was in short supply.

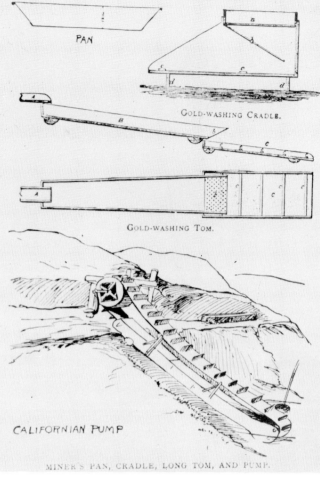

Gold-mining apparatus.

Closeup of a nozzle (also called a giant or monitor). Water is forced through at tremendous pressure and directed at the hillside. The nozzle can be raised or lowered with rock weights, and it swivels from side to side.

A modern mining method on Bonanza Creek. Many old claims are again being worked to wrest away gold the oldtimers overlooked.

Today several commercial outfits allow tourists to pan for gold on Bonanza Creek.

MINING AREAS

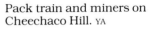

CHEECHAKO HILL
SEASONED SOURDOUGHS CHIDED NEWCOMER
OLIVER MILLETT FOR SEEKING GOLD ON A
HILL BECAUSE THE CREEKS WERE ALL
STAKED. THEY NAMED IT CHEECHAKO HILL,
BUT MILLETT PERSISTED AND FOUND GOLD
IN AN ANCIENT CREEK BED, THE WHITE
CHANNEL, 300' ABOVE THE LAUGHING MINERS
ON BONANZA CREEK.

Pack train and miners on Cheechaco Hill. YA

Cheechaco Hill turned out to be the richest hill deposit of them all. The old-timers could not believe that there was gold above the valley floor until Oliver Millett made the initial discovery in an ancient stream channel. UW CANTWELL

Long sluice boxes and dumps on Cheechaco Hill.
BETTMANN ARCHIVE/NEW YORK

Gold Hill, like the other worked-over hills above Bonanza Creek, is so overgrown today that it is hard to imagine the activity that went on here.

Extensive workings on Gold Hill. These bench deposits on ancient stream channels proved to be as rich as the lower stream claims. UW CURTIS

Dick Lowe's fraction on Bonanza Creek. Lowe was a chainman for the government surveyor, William Ogilvie. They measured Claim #2 Above and found it to be 78 feet too long. Lowe staked the excess for himself. He tried to sell it for $900, or get someone to work it, but everyone thought it too small to be worth working. Lowe finally worked it himself and it turned into the richest piece of ground in the entire Klondike country.

Grand Forks, the largest town in the mining area, was at the junction of Bonanza and Eldorado creeks. Thousands of people lived and worked in the vicinity. UW CURTIS

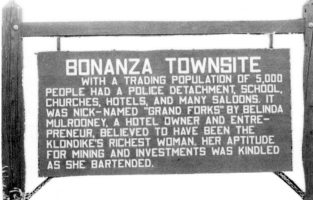

BONANZA TOWNSITE WITH A TRADING POPULATION OF 5,000 PEOPLE HAD A POLICE DETACHMENT, SCHOOL, CHURCHES, HOTELS, AND MANY SALOONS. IT WAS NICK-NAMED "GRAND FORKS" BY BELINDA MULROONEY, A HOTEL OWNER AND ENTRE-PRENEUR, BELIEVED TO HAVE BEEN THE KLONDIKE'S RICHEST WOMAN. HER APTITUDE FOR MINING AND INVESTMENTS WAS KINDLED AS SHE BARTENDED.

With the gold deposits being discovered farther and farther away from Dawson, many businesses, services and even churches were set up on the creeks to take care of the miners. One wonders how many people went to this church in Grand Forks. UW HEGG

This was Belinda Mulroney's establishment at Grand Forks. She became the richest woman in the Klondike by her shrewd business dealings. She opened a fancy hotel in Dawson, acquired numerous mining properties and eventually married a count and traveled to Europe. UW HEGG

Every conceivable service was performed on the creeks. A lot of people became rich without mining gold. This lady was probably very popular for her sewing and laundering. UW HEGG

Grand Forks is not even a ghost town today. The dredges have taken away all signs of this metropolis of the creeks.

In this 1976 photo the Klondike River and Bonanza Creek valleys still show considerable effects of the dredging operations. Dredges operated in the area from 1905 until 1959.

The road through the Bonanza Creek valley. This was some of the richest ground in the world and has been mined for more than 80 years, with gold still being found. The gravel piles are remains of the dredging operations that have changed the features of the countryside.

The white channel, or ancient stream beds, 100 to 300 feet above the present creek beds and up to two miles wide, is composed of pulverized talc and white quartz gravels. It held a great amount of gold, but was not discovered until after the creek beds had been staked. It is seen here on Bonanza Creek, where it has been hydraulically mined.

WHITE CHANNEL
AN ANCIENT HIGH-LEVEL RIVERBED UP TO 2 MILES WIDE, COMPOSED OF PULVERIZED TALC AND SHINING WHITE QUARTZ GRAVELS THAT CARRIED A BRIGHT GOLD IN GREAT QUANTITIES, IS FIRST SEEN HERE. IT WAS FOUND ON MANY HILLS IN THE KLONDIKE REGION AND ELUDED THE EARLIEST CREEKBED MINERS.

GOLD BOTTOM
THE COMMUNITY OF GOLD BOTTOM WAS ESTABLISHED AT THIS POINT, THE JUNCTION OF GOLD BOTTOM AND HUNKER CREEKS. IT BOASTED SUCH AMENITIES AS A SCHOOL, CHURCHES, HOTELS, N.W.M.P. BARRACKS, STORES, AND A MINING RECORDER'S OFFICE. THE TOWN WAS THE TRADING AND ENTERTAINMENT CENTER FOR THIS AREA.

HUNKER CREEK
ALBERT HUNKER STAKED THE FIRST CLAIM ON THIS CREEK SEPTEMBER 11, 1896. BOB HENDERSON WAS MINING ON A TRIBUTARY OF HUNKER WHEN CARMACK MADE THE BIG DISCOVERY ON BONANZA CREEK. AUGUST 17, 1896. HUNKER CREEK IS 18 MILES LONG, OF WHICH 13 MILES WERE DREDGED BETWEEN 1908 AND 1966.

CHAPTER EIGHT

AFTER THE RUSH

When gold was discovered on the beaches of Nome, Alaska, in July, 1899, the Klondike gold rush was over. In a few short weeks, after word spread to Dawson, thousands of miners departed for the new "Eldorado." Several more gold strikes were to occur in Alaska in the early 1900s but none ever equaled the Klondike.

Millions of dollars have been extracted from the creeks in the past 80-odd years, making the Klondike surely one of the largest and most durable gold fields in the world. Even today there is some gold production as individuals work old claims.

In the early 1900s hydraulic mining was conducted on the benches and hillside areas. Large nozzles, called giants or monitors, directed water under great pressure against the overburden and gold-laden gravels, washing them into sluice boxes where the gold was extracted. This was a cheap and effective way of mining low-grade gold gravels, but it took tremendous amounts of water and devastated the terrain.

In 1905 dredges were brought in to work the creeks and the Klondike River area. The dredges were able to process deposits of gravel after the ground in the creek areas was thawed by steam or—later—by cold water. Because of the natural thawing action of the stream and the absence of large boulders, dredging was easier on the Klondike River than on the creeks. The dredges worked 24 hours a day until the weather froze the water.

The huge gravel piles seen in the mining areas today are leftovers of these dredging operations, which finally ceased in 1966.

After 1900 transportation and communications improved greatly between Dawson and the

Dredge #4 was built in 1912 and was the largest wooden-hull, bucket-line dredge in North America. It worked in the Klondike Valley area until 1959. It was electrically operated and was 140 feet long, 65 feet wide and 76 feet high. It had 75 16-cubic-foot buckets and averaged between 8,000 and 10,000 cubic yards of gravel processed daily from April to November. In 1939, 35,000 ounces of gold were recovered with a value at the time of one million dollars.
UW CANTWELL

The method used for thawing the frozen ground in the stream valleys before a dredge could begin operation. Steam points were driven into the ground and the steam from large boilers would thaw it. This was not necessary in the Klondike River bed because of its natural thawing. Later it was found that cold water was a better thawing agent. UW CANTWELL

surrounding creeks and Whitehorse. The White Pass and Yukon Railway was completed to Whitehorse in July 1900, and provided easy access to the interior of the Yukon. A stage line was established between Whitehorse and Dawson, using sleds in the winter and wagons in the summer. With the completion of the Alaska Highway in 1942 and the resulting network of roads built into the interior, Dawson and other parts of the Yukon were much more accessible to miners, businessmen and tourists. Air travel has greatly expanded the accessibility of the country.

The Klondike Mines Railway was built from Dawson to the gold fields in 1906 and this facilitated the transport of supplies and gold to and from the area. The railway ran to Sulphur Springs. It was shut down in 1914 because of slackening gold production and rising costs.

Dawson went from its days as a boom town in 1897-99 to a new and stable life marked by steady improvements and a fairly constant population. The citizens who stayed behind when the Nome rush started could see that mining would produce a steady income, and they proceeded to build Dawson into one of the finest cities of the North. The Canadian government, sensing that the city would prosper, set up governmental offices and erected many fine buildings that are still used today. Men were joined by their families, schools were established, and paved streets, sewers, water lines and many shops were built. They gave Dawson the air of a normal town, even though it was many hundreds of miles from any other urban civilization.

But the decline of gold production after 1914, the depression of the 1930s and World War II almost turned Dawson into a ghost town. The territorial government was finally moved to Whitehorse in 1953. The population dwindled to about 700. Dawson has once again become alive with an increase in tourism and inclusion of part of the town in a national historical park.

Dredging operation from the mouth of the Klondike River to Bear Creek.
YA DOODY 1913

Bonanza Basin at the Ogilvie Bridge just south of Dawson, August 25, 1913. YA DOODY 1913

Panorama of the Klondike River Valley near its junction with Bonanza Creek in 1913. Joe Boyle's CKM Company dredges are in the foreground. Ogilvie Bridge and buildings in Gugglieville are shown.
YA DODDY 1913

Canadian Dredge No. 4.
YA

Crew members on the rear of a gold dredge. Note the water pouring out the sluice boxes, the final depository of the placer gold as it went through the entire dredging process. YA

By 1922, the area in the photo had been completely dredged and extensive tailing (gravel) piles had been left by the dredges. By the time dredging ceased in 1966, the terrain of hundreds of miles of streams had been completely changed. YA

Dredge #4 as it looked in the 1980s. It sunk in 16 to 18 feet of muck on Claim #17 Below Discovery on Bonanza Creek. It has been extensively remodeled through the years. In 1991–92 it was raised from the muck, cleaned up and put on display by Parks Canada. Much of the tools and machinery was found to be in good shape, preserved by the frozen ground.

BEAR CREEK

Bear Creek, a tributary of the Klondike, was first staked by Solomon Marpak in 1896. In the early days of the twentieth century, it became a center for the large dredging operations on the Klondike River and its gold-bearing tributaries. It was the headquarters for the giant Yukon Consolidated Gold Corporation until it ceased operation in 1966. The site is now owned by Parks Canada.

Hydraulic mining in the Klondike country in the early 1900s. This type of mining drastically changed the looks of the area in the years after the first rush was over. YA

Carcross in 1922 was a major stopping point on the White Pass and Yukon Route and a major Indian village in the Yukon. AMHA

Skagway in the 1930s was only a shadow of its former gold rush days. The Great Depression of the 1930s had been hard on the town and railroad. There was some tourist business from tour boats docking at Skagway and then transporting people over the rails to Whitehorse. BETTMANN ARCHIVE/NEW YORK

After 1900 Dawson settled down to a fairly stable economy of gold mining by large companies and as the government center for the Yukon Territory. The top photo was taken about 1908, the bottom in the late 1920s.
BETTMANN ARCHIVE/NEW YORK, YA

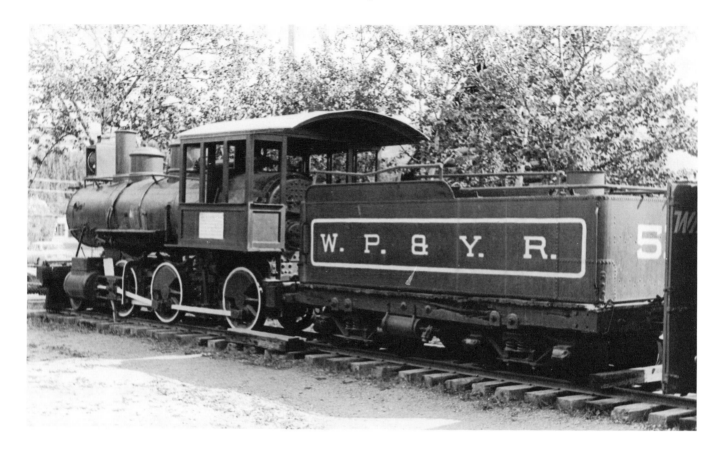

One of White Pass' steam engines is now on display at Whitehorse's MacBride Museum.

The Klondike Mines Railway ran from Klondike City 31 miles to Dome Mountain. It started operations in 1906 to haul supplies and passengers to the dredge and hydraulic operations. Due to large losses it ceased business in 1914. YA

BADGE OF YUKON
ORDER OF PIONEERS

Few periods in the history of North America have spawned as many legends as the Klondike Gold Rush era. People were thrown together in a common cause — the search for gold. The rush brought out the best and the worst in the men and women who participated. The tales of their adventures, hardships, agonies and despairs have filled many books.

Some of the stories are true; some are myths, conceived in the fertile imaginations of the many writers who capitalized on the great adventure. There was much to write about, and many were the characters involved.

Nearly everyone had a nickname. Sometimes it was based on the person's appearance, sometimes on his or her conduct, sometimes on where he or she was from. The cast included the Evaporated Kid, Circle City Mickey, Siwash George, Dog Salmon Bob, Silent Sam Bonnifield, the Kansas City Kid, the Rag Time Kid, French Curley, Nelly the Pig, Limejuice Lil and Spanish Dolores—memorable names that left a lasting impression. Some stampeders would capitalize on their names for the rest of their lives. And for everyone who experienced the rush, life would never be the same again.

Every character, skill, weakness and calling— whether that of politician, banker, bartender, farmer, businessman, teacher, nurse, drunk, con-man, gambler, or prostitute—was shaped to a common dimension: the drive to get to the gold fields and strike it rich. For a few, the dream came true, but it was not always in the creeks that gold was found; sometimes it was found on the streets of Dawson.

Many notable people of the period made their way north. Jack London, the author and adventurer, crossed the Chilkoot and guided several

Robert Service in front of his cabin.

Robert Service, the bard of the Klondike, lived in this cabin on the east end of Dawson from November 1909, to June 1912. Service had come north in 1904 to work in a bank in Whitehorse. He was later transferred to Dawson to work in the Canadian Bank of Commerce. Most of his famous poems about the Yukon, such as "The Cremation of Sam Magee," "Dangerous Dan McGrew," and "Law of the Yukon," were written before he went to Dawson but he produced several more volumes while there. He left Dawson in 1912 and roamed the world, finally settling in France. He died in 1958. No other person put the mood of the gold rush into words as well as Service.

boats through Miles Canyon, but after arriving at Dawson, decided mining was not for him and returned to the outside. Robert Service, who became the best-known poet of the period, did not appear on the scene until ten years after the rush was over, but his poems portray events as if he had experienced them himself. Rex Beach and Nelly Bly were among other well-known writers who went to the Klondike.

For several characters from the American West, the Klondike gold rush was the last great adventure. Calamity Jane was there, along with the famous poet, scout and Indian fighter, Captain Jack Crawford. Crawford was a familiar figure on the streets of Dawson and was the most prominent person at the town's July 4 celebration in 1898. Jack Dalton, a well-known frontiersman, had been in the area for years and built several trails north from the Lynn Canal.

Many other people, who were to become famous after the rush, got their start in the Klondike. Alexander Pantages, who built a chain of movie theaters across the United States, was a waiter in Dawson and operated a successful theater there. Tex Rickard, who became manager of the Madison Square Garden and the best-known boxing promoter of his day, got his start in the gambling halls of Circle City and Dawson. Augustus Mack, the developer of the Mack Truck, and Sid Grauman, builder of Grauman's Chinese Theater in Hollywood, also sought early stakes in Dawson.

The dance hall girls became world-famous. Kitty Rockwell, later to be known as Klondike Kate; Diamond Tooth Lil, Sweet Marie, Cad

Wilson and many others made fortunes from the lonely free-spending miners. Many would marry the rich miners and travel the world with them, only to leave them as their fortunes waned.

Joe Boyle, a Canadian boxer, had a fantastic career. After the first rush was over he bought an enormous amount of claims and built the largest gold dredges in the world. He got rich on his "Boyle Concession," dredging many square miles of the area. He later became a World War I hero and a companion of the Queen of Rumania.

Tom Lippy, a former YMCA instructor in Seattle who had gone north early, was one of the first to disembark from the *Excelsior* with a fortune in gold. He took almost two million dollars from his claim on Eldorado Creek and sold out in 1903. He moved back to Seattle and became a leading citizen and philanthropist, but like most other stampeders was bankrupt when he died, in 1931.

Clarence Berry, a fruit farmer from Fresno, California, was one of the few who held onto his fortune. He had prospected at Fortymile without luck but was one of the first stakers on Bonanza Creek. He traded a half interest in his Bonanza claim for a half interest in a claim on Eldorado Creek, staked by another lucky miner, Antone Stander. The two claims together produced more than one million dollars for Berry, who moved on to the Fairbanks, Alaska, area where he made another fortune. He struck a third fortune in the California oilfields and died a rich man in 1931.

Belinda Mulroney, "the Queen of Grand Forks," had worked her way north from Scranton, Pennsylvania, operating restaurants, working on a ship, hauling timber to the creeks and

Arizona Charlie Meadows was a famous scout, Indian fighter and sharpshooter of the American West. He worked in several famous Wild West shows and trekked north over the Chilkoot Pass with a portable bar that he lost in a flood at Sheep Camp. He built the Palace Grand Theater in Dawson from two wrecked river boats and was one of the richest and best-known promoters of the day. He is shown in the center of the photo. UW HEGG 1899

YA

finally opening a hotel at Grand Forks. She made money through shrewd investments and became a mining manager. In 1900 she married a count from France and they toured Europe. After some time in the Fairbanks area they moved to Yakima, Washington, and lived in style until the count was killed during World War I while on an inspection trip to France.

The four men most responsible for the first discovery of gold lived out their lives in different ways. Robert Henderson was finally recognized as a co-discoverer of the Klondike and the Canadian government gave him a small pension. He continued prospecting for the rest of his life, never finding the big strike. He died in 1931.

George Carmack divorced his Indian wife in 1900 and married again. He made good investments and when he died in 1922, left his second wife a large estate. Skookum Jim continued prospecting in the North until he wore himself out and died in 1916. Tagish Charley sold his mining properties and spent the rest of his days at Carcross, Yukon. He drowned after falling off a bridge on one of his drunken sprees.

This is the law of the Yukon, and
    ever she makes it plain:
Send not your foolish and feeble;
    send me your strong and sane—
Strong for the red rage of battle;
    same, for I harry them sore;
Send me men grit for the combat,
    men who are grit to the core;
Swift as the panther in triumph,
    fierce as the bear in defeat,
Sired of a bulldog parent, steeled
    in the furnace heat.
Send me the best of your breeding,
    lend me your chosen ones;
Them will I take to my bosom, them
    will I call my sons;
Them will I gild with my treasure,
    them will I glut with my meat;
But the others—the misfits, the
    failures—I trample under my feet.
Dissolute, dammed and despairful,
    crippled and palsied and slain,
Ye would send me the spawn of your
    gutters—Go! take back your spawn
    again.

*The Law of the Yukon—Robert Service

-188-

Jack Dalton, an early explorer of the Yukon, had constructed a trail from Pyramid Harbor on Lynn Canal to Fort Selkirk on the Upper Yukon River and charged a toll for its use. Thousands of cattle traversed it in 1898. YA

Inspector Charles Constantine was the first member of the North West Mounted Police to enter the wild Yukon Territory in 1894. He left the Yukon in 1898, at the height of the rush, for another assignment. AMHA

MOLLIE WALSH

Skagway has had its share of legendary characters, but few of them have been women. On Sixth Avenue, just off Broadway, stands a monument to one such lady—Mollie Walsh.

She arrived in Skagway from the brawling mining town of Butte, Mont., in October 1897. After spending the winter of 1897-98 in Skagway, she set up a grub tent that spring at Log Cabin along the White Pass Trail. There she served meals to miners passing along the trail.

Many admirers came to her tent door, one by the name of Jack Newman, an important packer on the trail. For a time, she and Newman saw a lot of each other, but she broke up with him after Newman shot a Skagway faro dealer in an argument over Mollie's affections. Mollie eventually married another well-to-do packer named Mike Bartlett, and the two of them moved to Dawson and later to Seattle.

In 1902, Bartlett murdered Mollie because of her affections for another man. Newman, who had never forgotten her, erected the monument in 1930 as a memorial to his former love.

Mollie Walsh's story is there for all to see to this day.

HARRIET PULLEN

As Skagway was at one time Alaska's largest city, it is only natural that Skagway was the site of Alaska's largest and most elaborate hotel—the Pullen House. Established by Mrs. Harriet Pullen a few years after the gold rush, it remained one of the North's leading hotels through the first half of this century.

Like thousands of other prospectors, Mrs. Pullen was lured north by the economic opportunities of the gold rush. She arrived in Skagway on Sept. 8, 1897, leaving behind a bankrupt farm and four children in Washington state. Her husband came north with her but the marriage eventually ended in divorce.

Mrs. Pullen first established a tent restaurant to feed Skagway's hungry stampeders, eventually moving the operation to a log building. Her apple pies soon made her quite a reputation, and she managed to save enough money to send for her three sons in Washington to help with the business.

In late 1897, she joined the rush to the newly found gold deposits at Atlin, British Columbia, but soon returned to her business in Skagway. Eventually, she saw an opportunity to provide the stampeders with transportation as well as food.

An experienced horsewoman, Mrs. Pullen still had seven horses down in Washington and knew she could put the animals to use packing prospectors and their supplies over the White Pass Trail. She sent for the horses, and when they arrived in Skagway she had to guide them to shore using a rowboat, as no one else would bring them in. She became one of the few women packers on the trail, and a particularly skillful one. The business, which she eventually sold, netted her a good stake for future enterprises. Her husband actually did most of the packing.

Her next project was a boarding house, and she rented a large frame house from Capt. Billy Moore. She later purchased the house and named it the Pullen House. Its tables were stocked with vegetables grown on land Mrs. Pullen owned near the old townsite of Dyea and with milk from her own cows.

Even in the years when the fortunes of Skagway were at a low ebb, the Pullen House was an outstanding hotel. For example, President Warren G. Harding visited the hotel on his 1923 trip to Alaska.

Mrs. Pullen became a well-known character throughout Alaska as well as in Skagway. She promoted tourism in Skagway, and amassed a vast collection of Alaskan artifacts. In her later years, she would relate to tourists the story of the shooting of Soapy Smith, an event she supposedly witnessed.

Two of her three sons, Dan and Royal, were decorated for valor during World War I, while her third son, Chester, drowned at Ketchikan when he was in his early 20s. After spending 50 years in her adopted town, Mrs. Pullen, a grand lady of the north, died in Skagway in 1947 at the age of 87.

The Pullen House finally succumbed to economic difficulties in the 1950s. Today, off of Broadway Street, one can still see its forlorn remains, the shell of what was once a glorious hotel.

Mrs. Pullen was an avid collector of historic Alaskana and was famous for her storytelling atributes. After her death, her granddaughter, Mary Pullen Kopanski of Seattle, Wash., exhibited the collection in Seattle from the late 1950s until it was sold by auction in 1973.

Mrs. Harriet Smith Pullen wearing her ermine coat and Indian garb, early 1900s. She had arrived in Skagway in 1897, and died there in 1947. AHL

Mrs. Pullen and her famous hotel, the Pullen House. The hotel had once been the residence of Captain Moore and his family. Through the years it was remodeled extensively. In the 1920s the Fifth Avenue Hotel was moved and connected to the hotel's north end. An enclosed porch was also added. The building is still standing but in disrepair.
D

SOAPY SMITH

Jefferson Randolph "Soapy" Smith probably ranks as Skagway's best-known character from the gold-rush days. Certainly, he was its most notorious con man. It is said that at the height of the gold rush, Smith and his gang virtually controlled the town, a reign that ended in a shoot-out with one of Skagway's leading citizens, Frank Reid.

Smith was born in Georgia in 1860 to parents who were both members of prominent Southern families. Smith spent most of his formative years in Texas, where his family moved in the 1870s. After his father, a lawyer, fell on hard times, young Jeff was forced to earn a living as a delivery boy and as a runner for a hotel, a job in which he rustled up customers and thus discovered his natural gift for speech.

While still in his teens, Smith hired on as a trail hand on cattle drives, and spent several years drifting about the West. He eventually learned sleight-of-hand tricks and made a living in the mining camps with gambling games such as the pea-under-the-shell game. He acquired his nickname "Soapy" from a game which involved hiding large bills in bars of soap.

Smith, who was generally opposed to violent methods, graduated to larger operations, and set up in Denver where he formed a gang. In Denver, he acquired a wide reputation for his con games as well as for his generosity to charities, churches, and those in desperate need. Also in Denver,

Jefferson Randolph "Soapy" Smith.

he married a singer by the name of Anna Nielsen, whom he kept insulated from his "public" life and who eventually bore his children.

About 1890, Smith set up operations, including a gambling hall, in Creede, Colo., a wide-open mining town, but eventually returned to Denver. After numerous run-ins with the law and local politicians, Soapy Smith quit Colorado and, in October 1897, arrived with his gang in Skagway, apparently with intentions of "taking over" the town.

Working out of an establishment called Jeff Smith's Parlor, an oyster parlor that also offered liquor and gambling, Smith and his gang soon were operating their con games, as well as taking part in some outright robbery, running a protection racket, and overseeing businesses like Smith's "Telegraph Office." This last business, which charged $5 to send a message anywhere in the world, might have been legitimate but for the fact that Skagway had no telegraph lines.

Despite his lawless ways, Smith was liked and respected by many for his charity, which included organizing a program to adopt stray dogs. The townspeople, however, had no use whatsoever for his gang. Eventually, several of Skagway's leading citizens formed a vigilante-style "Committee of 101" to rid the town of its criminal element. Among the committee's founders was 54-year-old Frank Reid, a former Indian fighter and surveyor who helped lay out the original town.

The showdown between Soapy Smith and Frank Reid began when a young miner, J.D. Stewart, arrived in Skagway from the Klondike carrying $2,700 in gold. Somehow, and apparently with the help of someone, Stewart and his gold parted ways. The Committee of 101, hearing Stewart's loud complaints, suspected Soapy Smith and his gang and on July 8, 1898, called a meeting on the Skagway wharf to take action.

Soapy Smith tried to force his way into the meeting, but found his path along the wharf blocked by Frank Reid. After a brief struggle the two exchanged gunfire and both fell to the deck. Smith died immediately of a bullet through the heart; Reid lingered 12 days longer.

With the death of Soapy Smith, the law-abiding citizens of Skagway got rid of other members of the gang. Most of them were shipped south, and many served time in prison. Smith and Reid were buried near each other in the Skagway cemetery, with Reid's tombstone bearing the words, "He gave his life for the Honor of Skagway." Soapy Smith's tombstone became a favorite among souvenir seekers, who believed a piece of the stone would bring them good luck.

Jeff Smith's Parlor was constructed in 1897 as a bank building. It later became Soapy Smith's saloon and headquarters and after his death a restaurant. Martin Itjen moved it across Sixth Avenue in 1935 and George Rapuzzi moved it to its present location on Second Avenue in 1964. It was operated for years by Itjen and Rapuzzi as a museum.

Smith and his cronies posing at a bar. Notice the Cuban-American flag picture on the wall. Smith formed a company of volunteers in the summer of 1898 to fight the Spaniards but the U.S. Army refused his services. AHL 1898

The shootout on the Skagway wharf on July 8, 1898. BODDY

Collage of the encounter between Soapy
Smith and Frank Reid on July 8, 1898.
AHL 1898

Some of the vigilantes from
Skagway who finally broke up
Smith's gang. AMHA

Funeral of Frank Reid, the killer
of Soapy Smith. AMHA

Top: Soapy Smith's grave at the Gold Rush Cemetery north of Skagway.

Bottom left: Frank Reid's grave marker at the Gold Rush Cemetery. His grave site is well kept compared to Smith's.

Bottom right: Frank Reid

Big Alex McDonald was known as the "King of the Klondike." He had arrived on the scene early and had grown rich buying property. He could not keep track of his many claims and he did not know how much he was worth, professing more interest in how many claims he could buy than in how many millions were his. He was a big, awkward man who had people bothering him constantly because he was so rich. Like most of the other stampeders, however, he died broke. BODDY

A few men who made it to Dawson were not interested in making money or living it up. One of these was Father Judge, a Jesuit priest, who was called the "Saint of the Klondike" for his humanitarian efforts. He founded a hospital where he worked night and day caring for the sick during the hectic winter of 1897-98. He looked much older than his 45 years, and when his constant work finally killed him, his death was mourned throughout the Yukon. BODDY

One of the best-known stories of the era concerns Swiftwater Bill Gates, a rich and ostentatious Dawson character, and his favorite dance-hall girl, 19-year-old Gussie Lamore. Gussie was fond of fresh eggs, which were scarce in Dawson. Bill was in a restaurant having breakfast when Gussie walked in on the arm of a gambler. She sat down and ordered the most expensive item on the menu—fried eggs. In a fit of jealousy, Bill went out and bought every egg in Dawson. He brought them back to the restaurant, had them fried one at a time, and threw them out to dogs in the street. While this makes for a good story it could be a figment of someone's imagination. The story does fit, however, the type of characters who lived and worked in the Dawson area during the height of the gold rush. BODDY

Poker was one of the main attractions in the gambling halls of Dawson. The stakes sometimes exceeded $50,000, and many a gambling hall was won or lost at the poker table. Men such as Silent Sam Bonnifield, Louis Golden and the Montana Kid played for days, winning and losing many fortunes. BODDY

Ladies of the night enjoying themselves in front of their cribs at White Chapel or Klondike City. There have been camp followers in every gold rush and mining town, and the Klondike was no exception.
UW L & D

Diamond Tooth Lil was another well-known dance hall girl in Dawson. Girls of every description and character worked in Dawson and their names are forever etched in the history of the period. YA

Klondike Kate was one of the most famous of the dance hall girls of Dawson. She often wore expensive gowns and a headdress of lighted candles. After the rush was over she went on the lecture circuit, telling of her life during the gold rush days. She died a recluse in Oregon in 1957. YA 1900

Lucille Elliot, also known as "Swedish Queen."
AMHA

"One of the Girls." YA

Interior of the MacBride Museum in Whitehorse. This plus gold rush museums in Skagway and Dawson portrays the history of the Klondike Gold Rush in a very graphic way. GOVERNMENT OF THE YUKON

CHAPTER TEN

LEGACY OF THE GOLD RUSH

The National Park Service's Skagway Visitors Center is now located in the 1898 White Pass and Yukon Route depot. Next door is the ornate 1900 railroad general office building, which is now the administrative offices for the Park Service. The building has been completely restored.

Exterior and interior views of the National Park Service's Klondike Gold Rush National Historical Park Visitor's Center at 117 South Main Street, Seattle, Wash. This center, along with the Skagway Unit of the park, is preserving as much as possible of this historic era. Parks Canada also has historic sites at Whitehorse and Dawson.

COURTESY NPS, KGRHP, SEATTLE

BIBLIOGRAPHY

Becker, Ethel Anderson, *Klondike 98, Hegg's Album of the 1898 Alaska Gold Rush*, Binfords & Mort, Portland, Oregon, 1949.

Berton, Pierre, *Klondike, The Last Great Gold Rush, 1896-1899*, McClelland and Stewart Ltd., Toronto, Ontario, 1972.

_____,*The Klondike Quest, A Photographic Essay, 1897-1899*, Little Brown and Co., Boston, Massachusetts, 1983

Bronson, William, *The Last Grand Adventure, The Story of the Klondike Gold Rush & the Opening of Alaska*, McGraw-Hill Book Co., New York, 1977.

Clifford, Howard, *The Skagway Story*, Alaska Northwest Publishing Co., Anchorage, Alaska., 1975.

_____, *Doing the White Pass*, Sourdough Enterprises, Seattle, Washington, 1983.

Green, Lewis, *The Gold Hustlers*, Alaska Northwest Publishing Co., Seattle, Washington, 1977.

Lung, Edward Burchall, *Black Sand and Gold*, 1956.

Morgan, Murray, *One Man's Gold Rush, A Klondike Album*, University of Washington Press, Seattle, 1967.

Robertson, Frank G. and Beth Kay Harris, *Soapy Smith, King of the Con Men*, Hastings House, New York, 1961.

Satterfield, Archie, *Chilkoot Pass: Then and Now*, Alaska Northwest Publishing Co., Anchorage, Alaska, 1973.

Sawatsky, Don, *Ghost Town Trails of the Yukon*, Stagecoach Publishing Co., Langley, British Columbia, 1975.

Spude, Robert L., *Chilkoot Trail*, University of Alaska, Fairbanks, 1980.

Summer, Harold Merritt, *This Was Klondike Fever*, Superior Publishing Co., Seattle, Washington, 1978.

Winslow, Kathryn, *Big Pan-Out: The Story of the Klondike Gold Rush*, W.W. Norton & Co., New York, 1951.

Wright, Allen A., *Prelude to Bonanza, The Discovery and Exploration of the Yukon*, Gray's Publishing Ltd., Sidney, British Columbia, 1976.